CONTENTS

Targeting English Homework
Year 4

ISBN: 978 1 925726 61 9

Published by Pascal Press
PO Box 250
Glebe NSW 2037
www.pascalpress.com.au
contact@pascalpress.com.au

Author: Norah Colvin
Publisher: Lynn Dickinson
Editor: Marie Theodore
Cover Designer: Janice Bowles
Typesetter: Stacey Grainger
Images & Illustrations: Dreamstime (unless otherwise indicated)

Acknowledgements
Thank you to the publishers, authors and illustrators who generously granted permission for their work to be reproduced in this book.

Introduction

Targeting English Homework aims to build and reinforce English skills. This book supports the ACARA V9 Australian Curriculum for Year 4 and helps children to revise and consolidate what has been taught in the classroom. ACARA codes are shown on each unit, and a chart explaining their content descriptions is on pages v and vi. The inside front and back covers show the topics in each unit.

The structure of this book

This book has 32 carefully graded double-page units which are divided into three sections:

- Reading & Comprehension – includes a wide variety of literary and cross-curriculum texts
- Grammar & Punctuation
- Phonic & Word Knowledge.

Each unit also includes a Reading Review segment for children to record and rate their home reading books.

What I'm reading

Title: ______________________

It's: ☐ a paper book/magazine/comic
☐ an audiobook
☐ online

It's: ☐ imaginative ☐ informative

Rating ☆☆☆☆☆

Reviews

The last unit in each term features a Review where children are encouraged to consider their opinion of a popular TV show, movie, computer game or book. They are asked in-depth questions about the subject over 4 pages. As responses will vary widely, there are no answers provided for these units (8, 16, 24 and 32). These Reviews are a great way to foster critical thinking skills and encourage reflection.

Assessment

Term Reviews follow Units 1–8, 9–16, 17–24 and 25–32 to test work covered during the term and allow parents and carers to monitor their child's progress. Children are encouraged to mark each unit as it is completed and to colour in the traffic lights at the end of each segment. These results are then transferred to the Marking Grid. Parents and carers can see at a glance if their child is excelling or struggling!

- **Green** = Excellent — 2 or fewer questions incorrect
- **Orange** = Passing — 50% or more questions answered correctly
- **Red** = Struggling — fewer than 50% correct and needs help

SCORE /18 0-6 8-14 16-18 *Score 2 points for each correct answer!*

How to Use This Book

The activities in this book are specifically designed to be used at home with minimal resources and support. Helpful explanations of key concepts and skills are provided throughout the book to help understand the tasks. Useful examples of how to do the activities are provided.

Regular practice of key concepts and skills will support the work your child does in school and will enable you to monitor their progress throughout the year. It is recommended that children complete 8 units per school term (one a week) and then the Term Review. Every unit has a Traffic Light scoreboard at the end of each section.

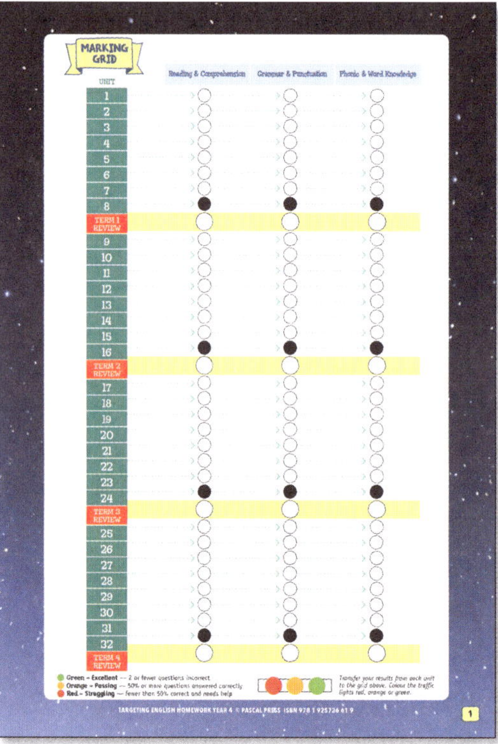

SCORE /18 0-6 8-14 16-18

Score 2 points for each correct answer!

You or your child should mark each completed unit and then colour the traffic light that corresponds to the number of correct questions. This process will enable you to see at a glance how your child is progressing and to identify weak spots. The results should be recorded at the end of each term on the Marking Grid on page 1. The Term Review results are important for tracking progress and identifying any improvements in performance. If you find that certain questions are repeatedly causing difficulties and errors, then there is a good reason to discuss this with your child's teacher and arrange for extra instruction in that problem area.

Home Reading Journal

Each unit provides space for your child to log, review and rate a book they have read during the week. These details can then be transferred to the handy Reading Journal Summary on page 146, which can be photocopied and shared with their teacher or kept as a record.

Answers

The answer section on pages 147–162 can be removed, stapled together and kept somewhere safe. Use it to check answers when your child has completed each unit. Encourage your child to colour in the Traffic Light boxes when the answers have been calculated.

TARGETING ENGLISH HOMEWORK YEAR 4 © PASCAL PRESS ISBN 978 1 925726 61 9

Australian Curriculum Correlations: Year 4 English

CODE	CODE DESCRIPTION	Reading & Comprehension UNITS	Grammar & Punctuation UNITS	Phonic & Word Knowledge UNITS
LANGUAGE				
AC9E4LA02	identify the subjective language of opinion and feeling, and the objective language of factual reporting		4, 8, 12, 16, 20, 24, 32	
AC9E4LA03	identify how texts across the curriculum have different language features and are typically organised into characteristic stages depending on purposes	1, 2, 3, 4, 5, 6, 7, 9, 10, 11, 12, 13, 14, 15, 17, 18, 19, 20, 21, 22, 23, 25, 26, 27, 28, 29, 30, 31		
AC9E4LA04	identify how text connectives including temporal and conditional words, and topic word associations are used to sequence and connect ideas		7, 11, 13, 22, 23, 25, 29	
AC9E4LA05	identify text navigation features of online texts that enhance readability including headlines, drop-down menus, links, graphics and layout	14		
AC9E4LA06	understand that complex sentences contain one independent clause and at least one dependent clause typically joined by a subordinating conjunction to create relationships, such as time and causality		1, 2, 3, 5, 9, 10, 11, 14, 15, 17, 20, 21, 22, 29	
AC9E4LA07	investigate how quoted (direct) and reported (indirect) speech are used		3, 15, 19, 23, 25, 31	
AC9E4LA08	understand how adverb groups/phrases and prepositional phrases work in different ways to provide circumstantial details about an activity		6, 17, 21, 27	
AC9E4LA09	understand past, present and future tenses and their impact on meaning in a sentence		2, 7, 18, 26, 30	
AC9E4LA10	explore the effect of choices when framing an image, placement of elements in the image and salience on composition of still and moving images in texts	5, 6, 13, 28, 32		
AC9E4LA11	expand vocabulary by exploring a range of synonyms and antonyms, and using words encountered in a range of sources		12, 18, 19, 20, 22, 26, 27, 31	
AC9E4LA12	understand that punctuation signals dialogue through quotation marks and that dialogue follows conventions for the use of capital letters, commas and boundary punctuation		1, 2, 3, 9, 13, 14, 18, 19, 21, 23, 25, 26, 28, 30, 31	
LITERATURE				
AC9E4LE02	describe the effects of text structures and language features in literary texts when responding to and sharing opinions	4, 8, 24		
AC9E4LE03	discuss how authors and illustrators make stories engaging by the way they develop character, setting and plot tensions	8, 11, 16, 19, 24		
AC9E4LE04	examine the use of literary devices and deliberate word play in literary texts, including poetry, to shape meaning		11, 19	19, 27
LITERACY				
AC9E4LY03	identify the characteristic features used in imaginative, informative and persuasive texts to meet the purpose of the text	1, 2, 3, 4, 5, 6, 7, 9, 10, 11, 12, 13, 14, 15, 17, 18, 19, 20, 21, 22, 23, 25, 26, 27, 28, 29, 30, 31		
AC9E4LY04	read different types of texts, integrating phonic, semantic and grammatical knowledge to read accurately and fluently, re-reading and self-correcting when needed	1, 2, 3, 4, 5, 6, 7, 8, 9, 10, 11, 12, 13, 14, 15, 17, 18, 19, 20, 21, 22, 23, 25, 26, 27, 28, 29, 30, 31		
AC9E4LY05	use comprehension strategies such as visualising, predicting, connecting, summarising, monitoring and questioning to build literal and inferred meaning, to expand topic knowledge and ideas, and evaluate texts	1, 2, 3, 4, 5, 6, 7, 9, 10, 11, 12, 13, 14, 15, 17, 18, 19, 20, 21, 22, 23, 25, 26, 27, 28, 29, 30, 31		
AC9E4LY06	plan, create, edit and publish written and multimodal imaginative, informative and persuasive texts, using visual features, relevant linked ideas, complex sentences, appropriate tense, synonyms and antonyms, correct spelling of multisyllabic words and simple punctuation		1, 2, 3, 4, 5, 6, 7, 12, 13, 14, 17, 18, 19, 21, 22, 23, 25, 26, 30, 31	
AC9E4LY09	understand how to use and apply phonological and morphological knowledge to read and write multisyllabic words with more complex letter combinations, including a variety of vowel sounds and known prefixes and suffixes			1, 2, 3, 4, 5, 6, 7, 9, 10, 11, 12, 13, 14, 15,17, 18, 20, 21, 22, 23, 25, 26, 27, 28, 29, 30, 31
AC9E4LY10	understand how to use knowledge of letter patterns, including double letters, spelling generalisations, morphological word families, common prefixes and suffixes, and word origins, to spell more complex words			2, 4, 5, 7, 9, 10, 12, 13, 15, 18, 19, 20, 21, 23, 25, 26, 28, 31
AC9E4LY11	read and write high-frequency words including homophones and know how to use context to identify correct spelling			3, 6, 11, 12, 15, 17, 19, 22, 23, 25, 26, 27, 31

Australian Curriculum Correlations: Year 4 English

CODE	CODE DESCRIPTION	Reading & Comprehension UNITS	Grammar & Punctuation UNITS	Phonic & Word Knowledge UNITS
CROSS CURRICULAR COMPREHENSION TEXTS				
HEALTH & PHYSICAL EDUCATION				
AC9HP4P08	describe and apply protective behaviours and help-seeking strategies in a range of online and offline situations	12, 14, 30		
AC9HP4P10	investigate and apply behaviours that contribute to their own and others' health, safety, relationships and wellbeing	12, 14, 30		
HASS INQUIRY AND SKILLS				
AC9HS4S03	interpret information and data displayed in different formats	18		
HISTORY				
AC9HS4K01	the diversity of First Nations Australians, their social organisation and their continuous connection to Country/Place	18, 21		
AC9HS4K02	the causes of the establishment of the first British colony in Australia in 1788	18		
AC9HS4K03	the experiences of individuals and groups, including military and civilian officials, and convicts involved in the establishment of the first British colony			
AC9HS4K04	the effects of contact with other people on First Nations Australians and their Countries/Places following the arrival of the First Fleet and how this was viewed by First Nations Australians as an invasion	18		
GEOGRAPHY				
AC9HS4K05	the importance of environments, including natural vegetation and water sources, to people and animals in Australia and on another continent	10, 21		
AC9HS4K06	sustainable use and management of renewable and non-renewable resources, including the custodial responsibility First Nations Australians have for Country/Place	12		
CIVICS AND CITIZENSHIP				
AC9HS4K07	the differences between "rules" and "laws", why laws are important and how they affect the lives of people	21		
AC9HS4K09	diversity of cultural, religious and/or social groups to which they and others in the community belong, and their importance to identity	21		
SCIENCE				
AC9S4U01	explain the roles and interactions of consumers, producers and decomposers within a habitat and how food chains represent feeding relationships	6, 12		
AC9S4U02	identify sources of water and describe key processes in the water cycle, including movement of water through the sky, landscape and ocean; precipitation; evaporation; and condensation	10, 14		
AC9S4U03	identify how forces can be exerted by one object on another and investigate the effect of frictional, gravitational and magnetic forces on the motion of objects	2, 22, 27, 28		
AC9S4U04	examine the properties of natural and made materials including fibres, metals, glass and plastics and consider how these properties influence their use	5, 28, 29		

Australian CURRICULUM

TARGETING ENGLISH HOMEWORK YEAR 4 © PASCAL PRESS ISBN 978 1 925726 61 9

MARKING GRID

UNIT	Reading & Comprehension	Grammar & Punctuation	Phonic & Word Knowledge
1			
2			
3			
4			
5			
6			
7			
8			
TERM 1 REVIEW			
9			
10			
11			
12			
13			
14			
15			
16			
TERM 2 REVIEW			
17			
18			
19			
20			
21			
22			
23			
24			
TERM 3 REVIEW			
25			
26			
27			
28			
29			
30			
31			
32			
TERM 4 REVIEW			

Green = **Excellent** — 2 or fewer questions incorrect
Orange = **Passing** — 50% or more questions answered correctly
Red = **Struggling** — fewer than 50% correct and needs help

Transfer your results from each unit to the grid above. Colour the traffic lights red, orange or green.

AC9E4LA03, AC9E4LY03, AC9E4LY04, AC9E4LY05

Imaginative text – Narrative

The Zipper

One Saturday, I helped Dad load up the trailer with junk to take to the tip. There was a lot of old stuff under the house, and everything was covered in a layer of dust. We carried out stacks of old books and jars and an old rusty bed.

Then we dragged Dad's old billycart out into the sunlight. It was really heavy. It had a coffin-shaped body made out of sheets of iron nailed over a wooden frame. Dad wiped some dust away. 'The Zipper' was painted on the side.

"I made this when I was about your age," said Dad. "It was the fastest thing around."

"You're not taking it to the tip, are you?" I said. "Can we keep it?"

Dad shook his head. "Too dangerous," he said.

I wiped off more dust. "Look at this!" I said, pointing at the yellow and red flames painted along each side. "Cool!"

"Please Dad, I won't drive it. I promise."

Dad thought for a moment. "OK, Nathan, you can keep it. But don't drive it on the road."

A couple of days later, Owen and Nick came round to my place. I was out the back working on The Zipper. I could see they were impressed.

"Let's give it a run," said Owen.

"Yeah," said Nick. "Let's go down Birdy Street!"

Source: Text adapted from *The Zipper* by David Dickson, Sparklers, Blake Education.

Reading & Comprehension

TERM 1

Shade the bubble next to the correct answer. Write the answer on the line where appropriate.

1. When does the story take place?
   - ◯ during the school holidays
   - ◯ on Saturday
   - ◯ on Sunday

2. Where does the story take place?
   - ◯ at school
   - ◯ at the tip
   - ◯ at Nathan's house

3. Who is the main character in the story?
   - ◯ Dad
   - ◯ Nathan
   - ◯ Owen
   - ◯ Nick

4. What were Nathan and Dad doing?
   - ◯ getting rid of junk
   - ◯ selling a trailer
   - ◯ repairing a billycart

5. What were Nathan and Dad going to do with the junk?
   - ◯ sell it on an online marketplace
   - ◯ take it to the tip
   - ◯ take it to a charity store

6. What did Nathan want to keep?
   - ◯ a coffin-shaped box
   - ◯ old books
   - ◯ a billycart

7. Why didn't Dad want to keep it?
   - ◯ It was old and dirty.
   - ◯ It was dangerous.
   - ◯ He didn't want Nathan to have fun.

8. What were the names of Nathan's friends?
   - ◯ Ted and Owen
   - ◯ Owen and Neil
   - ◯ Owen and Nick

9. What did they want Nathan to do with the billycart?
   - ◯ paint it
   - ◯ give it a run
   - ◯ sell it to them

10. What do you think Nathan will do now?

____

____

____

____

____

Why? ____

____

____

____

____

____

What I'm reading

Title: ______________________________

It's: ☐ a paper book/magazine/comic
☐ an audiobook
☐ online

It's: ☐ imaginative ☐ informative

Rating ☆ ☆ ☆ ☆ ☆

Score 2 points for each correct answer!

SCORE /20 0-8  10-14  16-20

Grammar & Punctuation

AC9E4LA06, AC9E4LA12, AC9E4LY06

TERM 1

Sentences

A sentence is a group of words that states a complete thought. It makes sense on its own.

A simple sentence has a subject and a verb.

Example: Dad wiped some dust away.

A statement is a sentence that tells us about everyday things, facts and ideas. It begins with a capital letter and ends with a full stop (.).

Underline the subjects and circle the verbs in these statements.

1. We carried out stacks of old books and jars.
2. Dad shook his head.
3. I wiped off more dust.
4. You can keep it.
5. Nick and Owen came round to my place.

Objects

Many sentences also contain an object. An object is someone or something that receives the action of the subject.

Example: Dad **wiped** some dust away.

subject

verb

object

Underline the objects in these statements.

6. We dumped stacks of old books and jars.
7. We dragged Dad's old billycart into the sunshine.
8. Dad shook his head.
9. Owen and Nick looked at The Zipper.
10. Dad made the billycart.

Questions

A question is a sentence that asks for information. It begins with a capital letter and ends with a question mark (?). Questions can begin with **who**, **what**, **which**, **how**, **when**, **where** or **why**.

Add a question word to complete these questions.

11. ____________ did Dad make the billycart?
12. ____________ are you taking the billycart to the tip?
13. ____________ can't I keep it?

Not all questions begin with those question words. Reread *The Zipper*. Write two questions you found in the story on these lines.

14. ____

____

____

15. ____

____

____

The verbs do, does, did, has, have, will and can are also useful for asking questions.

Complete these questions using one of these verbs.

16. __________ Nathan want to keep the billycart?
17. __________ Nathan's dad make the billycart?
18. __________ Nick and Owen seen the billycart before?
19. __________ Nathan's dad let him keep The Zipper?
20. __________ Nathan and his dad fix The Zipper?

Score 2 points for each correct answer!

SCORE /40

TARGETING ENGLISH HOMEWORK YEAR 4 © PASCAL PRESS ISBN 978 1 925726 61 9

Phonic & Word Knowledge

AC9E4LY09

TERM 1

Short vowel sounds – a, e, i, o, u

Say each word. They all contain a short vowel sound – the sound is short and snappy.

Dad	had	back	drag	stack
bed	help	then	red	let
tip	zip	Nick	with	this
lot	of	on	not	off
up	stuff	rust	but	junk

Choose words from the word bank to complete these sentences.

1. There were yellow and __________ flames painted on the side of the billycart.
2. Nathan had a friend called __________.
3. Nathan was helping Dad take the __________ to the tip.
4. There was a __________ of old junk under the house.
5. Nathan carried out a __________ of old books.

Some words have different ways of spelling the short vowel sounds.

Examples:

These words have the short **'e'** sound: h**ea**d, s**ai**d, h**ea**vy.

This word has the short **'i'** sound: g**i**ve.

This word has the short **'o'** sound: w**a**s.

This word has the short **'u'** sound: s**o**me.

Choose words from the box to complete these sentences.

6. The billycart was very __________.
7. "I made this when I was about your age," __________ Dad.
8. Owen wanted to __________ the billycart a run.
9. Dad said the billycart __________ old and dangerous.
10. The billycart was made from __________ sheets of iron.

Long vowel sounds – a, e, i, o, u

Long vowel sounds, in which the sound is the name of the letter, are often spelt with an **e** at the end of the word.

Examples: take wipe lone cute

However, long **e** is not often spelt with an **e** at the end, and there are other ways of spelling these long vowel sounds.

Say each word. They all contain a long vowel sound – the name of the letter.

a: take made frame place came age nail paint day they

e: we me see sheets keep street please each piece niece

i: wipe side drive bike slide mine my fly right pie

o: rope home note mole dome rose go road load

u: use fuse muse tube mule huge cube cute dune new

Choose a word from the box to match these meanings.

11. a border around a picture __________
12. a place where one lives __________
13. toothpaste comes in a __________
14. how old you are __________
15. the shape of a dice __________
16. a small part of something __________
17. transport with two wheels __________
18. most birds can do this __________
19. bed covers __________
20. a sweet smelling flower __________

Score 2 points for each correct answer! SCORE /40 0-18 20-34 

TERM 1

Informative text – Procedure

Marshmallow Popper

How can you make a marshmallow fly? This activity shows how the size of a force changes the distance an object travels.

What you need

- yoghurt cup
- scissors
- balloon
- mini marshmallows
- pavement chalk

What you do

1. Ask an adult to cut out the bottom of the yoghurt cup.
2. Tie a knot at the open end of the balloon and cut off about 1 cm from the other end.
3. Stretch the cut end of the balloon over the top rim of the yoghurt cup.
4. Go outside on a paved surface if possible. Drop a mini marshmallow into the cup, pull back on the knotted end of the balloon, aim into the distance, and let go.
5. How far did the marshmallow travel? Mark the place where it landed with pavement chalk. How can you make the distance longer or shorter? Test your idea. Mark each landing place.
6. Pulling back on the balloon and then letting go creates a force that pushes the marshmallow.

Source: *Targeting Science Year 4*, Pascal Press.

TARGETING ENGLISH HOMEWORK YEAR 4 © PASCAL PRESS ISBN 978 1 925726 61 9

Reading & Comprehension

TERM 1

Shade the bubble next to the correct answer. Write the answer on the line where appropriate.

1. **What is the purpose of this procedure?**
   - ◯ to make marshmallows
   - ◯ to make marshmallows fly
   - ◯ to toast marshmallows

2. **What will you learn about in this procedure?**
   - ◯ how good marshmallows taste
   - ◯ that marshmallows can fly
   - ◯ that the size of a force affects how far an object will travel

3. **Why do you need the scissors? (Choose any that apply.)**
   - ◯ to cut the bottom off the yoghurt cup
   - ◯ to cut your fingernails
   - ◯ to cut the end off the balloon

4. **Which of these is not part of the procedure? (Choose any that apply.)**
   - ◯ asking an adult for help
   - ◯ eating yoghurt
   - ◯ eating marshmallows

5. **Why do you need an adult's help?**
   - ◯ so you don't eat too many marshmallows
   - ◯ because it's tricky cutting the bottom out of a yoghurt cup
   - ◯ to measure how far the marshmallows fly

6. **Which of these things do you not do with the balloon?**
   - ◯ blow it up
   - ◯ tie a knot in the end
   - ◯ stretch it over the yoghurt cup

7. **Why is it helpful to do this activity on a paved area?**
   - ◯ so the marshmallows don't get lost in the grass
   - ◯ so you can draw a line where the marshmallows land
   - ◯ because it's a flat surface

8. **How do you make the marshmallow fly?**
   - ◯ You throw it into the air.
   - ◯ You put it inside the balloon and let it go.
   - ◯ You pull back on the balloon and let it go.

9. **Does the procedure tell you how far the marshmallows will fly?**
   - ◯ Yes
   - ◯ No
   - ◯ Unsure

10. **How far do you think a marshmallow will fly if you follow the procedure?**

    ____

    ____

    How could you check your answer?

    ____

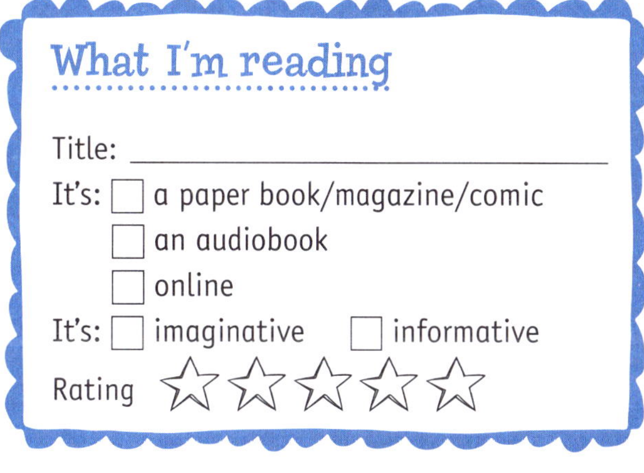

Score 2 points for each correct answer! SCORE /20   

Grammar & Punctuation

AC9E4LA06, AC9E4LA09, AC9E4LA12, AC9E4LY06

TERM 1

Simple sentences – Commands

Some sentences are commands. A command tells someone to do something. The subject of a command is always 'you'. Some commands have objects and some don't. Commands begin with a capital letter and end with full stop (.) or an exclamation mark (!).

Commands begin with a doing word or verb.

Examples: **Make** a marshmallow popper.
Watch the marshmallow fly!

The instructions in a procedure are a series of commands that begin with verbs.

Write a doing verb to complete these commands.

1. ____________ the bottom from the yoghurt cup.
2. ____________ a knot at the open end of the balloon.
3. ____________ a cross where the marshmallow lands.
4. ____________ how far the marshmallow will fly!
5. ____________ the leftover marshmallows!

Add words to these doing verbs to write commands. Use a full stop or exclamation mark at the end.

6. Run ____________
7. Cut ____________
8. Go ____________
9. Brush ____________
10. Find ____________

Exclamations

An exclamation is a sentence that shows surprise, fear, happiness or excitement.

Exclamations begin with a capital letter and end with an exclamation mark (!).

Sometimes, commands are exclamations.

Examples: It's not fair!
Mine flew the farthest!
Do it again!

Read these sentences. Write S for statement, Q for question, C for command or E for exclamation. Complete each sentence with the correct punctuation mark.

11. _____ We made a marshmallow popper_____
12. _____ What do you need to make a marshmallow popper_____
13. _____ That's the best so far_____
14. _____ How far did your marshmallow fly_____
15. _____ Pull back on the balloon and let it go_____

A command tells you what to do (future). A statement tells what you did (past).

Rewrite each of these commands as a statement to tell what you did. Each statement will begin with 'I' and use the past tense.

16. Tie a knot at the open end of the balloon.

____

____

17. Stretch the balloon over the rim of the yoghurt cup.

____

____

18. Go outside on a paved surface.

____

____

19. Mark each landing place.

____

____

20. Pull back on the balloon and let it go.

____

____

Score 2 points for each correct answer! SCORE /40  0-18  20-34  36-40

TARGETING ENGLISH HOMEWORK YEAR 4 © PASCAL PRESS ISBN 978 1 925726 61 9

AC9E4LY09, AC9E4LY10

Verb tenses – Adding 'ed' and 'ing'

For most verbs, when we change tense between past and present, we simply add 'ed' or 'ing' to the base verb.

Example: ask asked asking

When the base verb ends with 'e', we leave off the 'e' and add 'ed' or 'ing'.

Example: create created creating

When the base verb has one vowel followed by one consonant, we double the consonant before adding 'ed' and 'ing'.

Example: stop stopped stopping

Add endings to these base verbs to show past tense and present tense.

	Base verb	Did (past tense)	Doing now (present tense)
1	pull		
2	aim		
3	hop		
4	chase		
5	trade		
6	grab		
7	mark		
8	drop		
9	stretch		
10	joke		

Irregular verbs

Some verbs don't follow the usual pattern for past tense. Instead of adding 'ed', the verb changes.

Example: Today I **made**. I am **making**.
Yesterday I **made**.

Draw lines to match the base verb with its past tense verb.

11	go	let
12	cut	drove
13	let	went
14	eat	laid
15	drive	ate
16	lay	cut

In each sentence, one word is incorrect. Circle the word. Write the sentence correctly.

17 Placed the marshmallow in the yoghurt cup.

____

____

18 You stretching the balloon over the bottom of the cup.

____

____

19 The mark on the ground shows where the marshmallow landing.

____

____

20 The adult cutted the bottom off the yoghurt cup.

____

____

21 My marshmallow goed farther than yours.

____

____

22 I am test how to make the marshmallow fly farther.

____

____

Score 2 points for each correct answer!

SCORE /44    

AC9E4LA03, AC9E4LY03, AC9E4LY04, AC9E4LY05

Imaginative text – Narrative

Victim of Alien Abduction

Hamish has just discovered that, as nosebleeds are a sign of alien abduction, he may have been abducted by aliens. He goes to his friend Trev's house to tell him.

"Hey, Trev!" I called through the glass. Trev looked up from his computer and walked over to let me in. "Guess what!" I blurted.

He looked at me for a moment, probably noticing the crusted blood around my nostrils.

"Er, you've finally had your brain removed?"

"Ha, ha," I replied.

"So, what're you up to, Hamish?"

"Nothing much."

"Why are you here then?"

"Don't you want to guess?"

"I just did, and I wasn't right. So now you've gotta tell me."

"What?"

"Whatever it was I was supposed to be guessing."

"Oh, yeah."

I'd planned to tell him about my discovery but suddenly I wasn't so sure. What if he had been abducted too? Then a really chilling thought struck me: what if *he* were an alien? Trev sat at his desk, picking his nose thoughtfully, just looking at me. I wondered if he was communicating in some sort of secret code. Imagine that: an entire language made up of nose-picking actions. And what about him asking me if I'd had my brain removed? Wasn't that just a *bit* more than a coincidence? Maybe he knew more about my alien abduction than I did. I quickly changed the subject.

Source: Image and extract from *Nosebleed* by Ged Maybury, Blake Education.

TARGETING ENGLISH HOMEWORK YEAR 4 © PASCAL PRESS ISBN 978 1 925726 61 9

Reading & Comprehension

TERM 1

Shade the bubble next to the correct answer. Write the answer on the line where appropriate.

1. Where does the story take place?
   - ◯ at Hamish's house
   - ◯ at Trev's house
   - ◯ in an alien spaceship

2. Why did Hamish think he might have been abducted by aliens?
   - ◯ He saw a spaceship.
   - ◯ His friend Trev was acting weird.
   - ◯ His nose was bleeding.

3. What was Trev doing when Hamish arrived at his house?
   - ◯ playing a video game
   - ◯ something on his computer
   - ◯ picking his nose

4. What did Trev guess had happened to Hamish?
   - ◯ He'd been abducted by aliens.
   - ◯ He'd been picking his nose.
   - ◯ He'd had his brain removed.

5. Was it a serious guess?
   - ◯ Yes
   - ◯ No
   - ◯ Unsure

6. Why did he guess that?
   - ◯ He was really an alien.
   - ◯ He was working with the aliens.
   - ◯ He saw dried blood under Hamish's nose.

7. Why didn't Hamish tell Trev about his discovery?
   - ◯ He thought Trev might be an alien.
   - ◯ He was embarrassed.
   - ◯ He thought Trev was disgusting picking his nose.

8. How did Hamish think Trev might be communicating with the aliens?
   - ◯ on the computer
   - ◯ with nose-picking actions
   - ◯ writing coded messages in blood

9. What did Hamish think was too much of a coincidence?
   - ◯ Trev was picking his nose.
   - ◯ Trev was working on his computer.
   - ◯ Trev asked if Hamish had had his brain removed.

10. How do you think Hamish **discovered** that nosebleeds are a sign of alien abduction?

    ____

    ____

    Do you think he should trust the source?

    ____

    Explain:

    ____

    ____

    ____

    ____

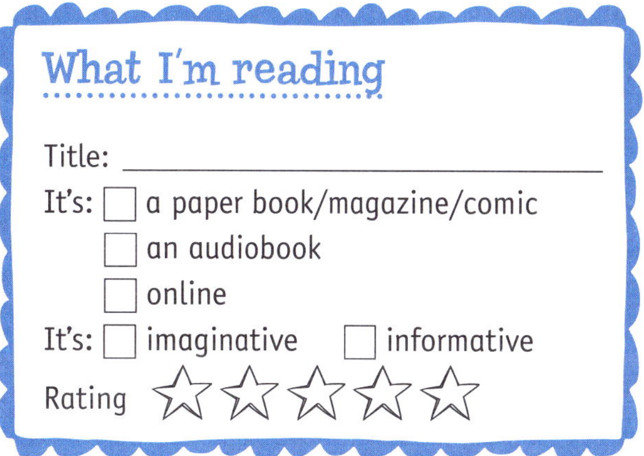

Score 2 points for each correct answer!

SCORE /20

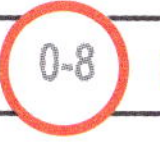

Grammar & Punctuation

AC9E4LA06, AC9E4LA07, AC9E4LA12, AC9E4LY06

Nouns – Common nouns

Common nouns are words used to name people, animals, places and things.

Common nouns are either concrete or abstract.

Concrete nouns name the things we can see, taste, hear and touch.

Examples: house, glass, alien, nose, blood, brain

Abstract nouns name ideas and feelings.

Examples: discovery, abduction, thought, guess, communication

Proper nouns are the names of particular people, places, objects and events. Proper nouns begin with a capital letter.

Examples: Hamish, Trev

Circle the nouns in this paragraph.

1 – 12 Hamish made a wild discovery. He found out that nosebleeds were a sign of alien abduction. He hurried to tell his friend Trev. Trev was picking his nose. Was it a coincidence? Could he be an alien? Hamish wasn't sure.

List the concrete nouns.

13 – 16

____

____

____

____

List the abstract nouns.

17 – 20

____

____

____

____

List the proper nouns.

21 – 22

____

____

Direct speech – Speech marks, commas, capital letters

Writers tell us what people say to each other by using speech marks (quotation marks). The speech marks ("...") go at the beginning and end of what was said. The first spoken word always has a capital letter. A comma marks off the spoken words from the rest of the sentence.

Example: "I have something to tell you," said Hamish.

speech marks — capital letter — comma — speech marks

Do not use a comma if the sentence has a question mark (?) or exclamation mark (!).

Add the missing capital letters, speech marks and other punctuation where necessary.

23 hey, Trev! I called through the glass.

24 have you had your brain removed asked Trev.

25 I've just made an amazing discovery said Hamish.

Saying verbs

Saying verbs show which people are talking and how they say things.

Examples: "Guess what!" I blurted.
"What are you up to?" asked Trev.

When two characters take turns to talk to each other, the writer doesn't always use saying verbs and the characters' names. The writer expects the reader to know who is talking by what is being said and whose turn it is.

Add saying verbs and names to show who is saying each of these sentences.

26 "So, what're you up to, Hamish?" ____________

27 "Nothing much," ____________

28 "Why are you here then?" ____________

29 "Don't you want to guess?" ____________

30 "I just did, and I wasn't right. So now you've gotta tell me," ____________

Score 2 points for each correct answer! SCORE /60

TARGETING ENGLISH HOMEWORK YEAR 4 © PASCAL PRESS ISBN 978 1 925726 61 9

Phonic & Word Knowledge

AC9E4LY09, AC9E4LY11

Apostrophes – Contractions and possession

Apostrophes are used in contractions. Contractions are two words shortened into one word. They are often used in speaking.

Examples: "**What're** you up to?" Trev asked. ("**What are** you up to?" Trev asked.)
"**You've** got to tell me," Trev said. ("**You have** got to tell me," Trev said.)

Apostrophes are also used to show possession or ownership.

Examples: Hamish**'s** nose Trev**'s** house

Watch out! Don't confuse it's and its.

It's is a contraction. It means it is or it has.

Example: **It's** the first day of the holidays. (**It is** the first day of the holidays.)

Its is a possessive pronoun. It is used to show possession.

Example: The alien departed in **its** spaceship. (its own spaceship, not it is spaceship)

Read these sentences. Circle the words with an apostrophe. Write C for contraction. Write P for possession.

1. _____ Hamish looked through the window of Trev's house.
2. _____ Trev looked at the dried blood around Hamish's nostrils.
3. _____ "You're scaring me," said Hamish.
4. _____ "I don't believe there are any aliens here," said Trev.
5. _____ The look on Trev's face was puzzling.
6. _____ Hamish wasn't sure if he should believe Trev or not.
7. _____ Hamish thought he'd been abducted by aliens because his nose was bleeding.
8. _____ "I've already guessed your brain has been removed," said Trev.
9. _____ "I'm sure Trev's one of them," thought Hamish.
10. _____ The alien's spaceship was nowhere to be seen.

Draw lines to match these contractions with their meanings.

11. what're	cannot
12. doesn't	you have
13. couldn't	could not
14. can't	what are
15. you've	I would
16. I'd	does not

Words that look alike but sound different

through: Hamish looked thr**ough** the window. (**ough** spells **'oo'** as in tr**ue** and m**oo**n)

thought: Hamish th**ough**t he'd been abducted. (**ough** spells **'or'** as in s**aw** and f**or**)

though: There was no proof th**ough**. (**ough** spells long vowel **'o'** as in g**o** and b**oa**t)

Choose the correct words to complete these sentences.

17. I _______________ I would write a story about aliens.
18. I looked _______________ a book to find an illustration.
19. I couldn't find one _______________.

On each line, circle the word that has a different vowel sound.

20. thr**ough**: blew moon you who two though
21. th**ough**t: brought sort sauce paw through corn
22. th**ough**: through go know boat rose toe
23. m**oo**n: fruit soup spoon true book chew
24. c**or**n: ball door through board cork four
25. r**o**se: soap do toe no goat show

Score 2 points for each correct answer! SCORE /50 0-22 24-44 46-50

Persuasive text – Book review

Runt

Author: Craig Silvey

Allen & Unwin, 2022

ISBN: 9781761067846

Runt is the story of a girl called Annie Shearer who lives on a sheep farm in Upson Downs in Australia. Annie adopts a stray dog named Runt and they become best friends.

In the years before he met Annie, Runt had become very fast and agile. Those skills helped him avoid capture by other people. They are also useful for herding sheep on the Shearer's farm.

When a greedy landowner threatens to take over the Shearer's farm, Annie enters Runt in a famous Dog Show in London. Annie knows that Runt is fast and agile enough to win, and the cash prize for first place will enable them to save their farm. The only trouble is, he won't obey Annie if anyone else is watching.

Can Annie and Runt overcome the obstacles, win the competition, and save her family's farm?

Runt is a story of kindness and friendship. It's about being true to yourself and bringing out the best in others. There are moments that warm your heart and moments that make you laugh out loud. It also has beautiful illustrations.

Runt won the CBCA Book of the Year Award for younger readers in 2023.

I give it 5 stars and recommend it for readers over 8.

Source: Image from *Runt* by Craig Silvey, Allen & Unwin.

Reading & Comprehension

Write your answers on the lines provided.

1. What is the title of the book?

2. Who wrote the book?

3. Who published the book? When?

4. What is the International Standard Book Number (ISBN)?

5. Who is the main character?

6. What do you know about the main character?

7. Who are some other characters in the book?

8. Write three words to describe the type of story.

9. Did the reviewer enjoy the book? How do you know?

10. Do you think you would like to read this book? Explain your reasons.

What I'm reading

Title ______

It's: ☐ a paper book/magazine/comic
☐ an audiobook
☐ online

It's: ☐ imaginative ☐ informative

Rating ☆☆☆☆☆

Score 2 points for each correct answer! SCORE /20    

Grammar & Punctuation

AC9E4LY06, AC9E4LA02

Proper nouns

Proper nouns are the names of particular people, places, objects and events. They are also used for the titles of books, movies and television shows. Proper nouns begin with a capital letter.

Examples: **R**unt, **A**nnie, **A**ustralia

Sort the proper nouns in the word box to complete the table. Then add one more proper noun to each list.

Runt Annie Shearer Upson Downs
Australia Dog Show London Easter
Craig Silvey CBCA Book of the Year Awards

People/Animals
1
2
3
4

Places
5
6
7
8

Events
9
10
11
12

Noun groups

A noun group is a group of words built around a noun. The noun is the main word and the words in the noun group give more information about the noun.

Example: **girl** called Annie Shearer

noun — noun group

Circle the nouns and underline the noun groups in these sentences. (Hint: There may be more than one in each sentence.)

13. Annie Shearer lives on a sheep farm in Upson Downs in Australia.
14. Those skills helped him avoid capture by other people.
15. A greedy landowner threatened to take over the Shearer's farm.
16. Annie entered Runt in a famous Dog Show in London.

Add words to these nouns to form noun groups.

17. dog ____________________
18. book ____________________
19. girl ____________________
20. show ____________________

Emotive words

In a book review, emotive words are used to convince the reader to feel the same way about the book as the writer does. The words will be positive if the writer enjoyed the book or negative if they did not enjoy it.

Examples: great, best, funny, worst, awful

List three phrases (groups of words) that tell you the writer enjoyed reading *Runt*.

21. ____________________
22. ____________________
23. ____________________

Read these emotive words. Use green to circle the positive words. Use red to circle the negative words.

24. funny
25. strange
26. boring
27. exciting
28. fantastic
29. unbelievable
30. dreadful
31. scary
32. horrible
33. great
34. best
35. worst
36. wonderful

Score 2 points for each correct answer! SCORE /72

Phonic & Word Knowledge

UNIT 4

AC9E4LY09, AC9E4LY10

TERM 1

Syllables

Syllables are chunks of sounds in words. We can tell how many chunks of sounds there are in a word by clapping the beats.

Examples:

One beat or syllable: Runt, dog, friends, sheep, win

Two beats or syllables: Annie, story, before, agile, enters

Three or more beats or syllables: Australia, landowner, overcome, obstacles, competition

How many syllables do each of these words have?

1. capture _____
2. people _____
3. laugh _____
4. competition _____
5. farm _____
6. cash _____
7. illustrations _____
8. give _____
9. Shearer _____
10. beautiful _____
11. recommend _____
12. trouble _____

The letter 'y'

The letter 'y' can be a consonant or a vowel.

When it is at the beginning of a word, it is usually a consonant. *Examples:* year, you

When it is at the end of a one-syllable word, it is usually a vowel and has a long 'i' sound. *Examples:* my, fly

When it is at the end of a two-syllable word, it is usually a vowel and has the long 'e' sound. *Examples:* very, greedy

Sometimes it works with other letters to make other long vowel sounds. It works with 'a' and 'e' in these words to make the long 'a' sound. *Examples:* day, stray, they, obey

Say each word. Underline the letter 'y'. Write C if it's a consonant or V if it's a vowel.

13. story _____
14. stray _____
15. only _____
16. any _____
17. yes _____
18. try _____
19. you _____
20. family _____
21. yak _____
22. busy _____
23. prey _____
24. yourself _____

Schwa sound

Words with two or more syllables have one or more stressed syllables and one or more unstressed syllables. The vowel in the unstressed syllable usually has the schwa sound. It sounds like 'uh'. There is no special letter to represent it in written words. You will only see the letters that represent the vowel sounds: a, e, i, o, u and y.

Say these words. Each word begins with an unstressed syllable and the schwa sound.

avoid about adopt
award alone approve around

Choose words from the box to complete these sentences.

25. Annie hopes Runt will win an _______________ at the Dog Show.
26. Runt learned to _______________ people for a long time.
27. The story is _______________ a girl and a dog.
28. The Shearers did not _______________ of what the greedy landowner wanted to do.

Say these words. Each word begins with a stressed syllable and the short 'a' sound.

agile apple anger
adult acid action angle

Choose words from the box to complete these sentences.

29. Runt was fast and _______________ enough to win the award at the Dog Show.
30. Annie was a child, but the greedy landowner was an _______________.

Score 2 points for each correct answer! SCORE /60   

AC9E4LA03, AC9E4LY03, AC9E4LY04, AC9E4LY05, AC9E4LA10, AC9S4U04

Informative text – Table

The World's Tallest Buildings

Designers use science, engineering and maths knowledge to make sure tall buildings stand safely. Not only do these towers have to be strong and stable, but they also have to hold an enormous amount of weight.

In 2023, seven of the world's ten tallest buildings were in Asia, with five of them in China. However, the world's tallest building was in the United Arab Emirates (UAE).

Australia's tallest building was the Q1 on the Gold Coast. It was completed in 2005. It is 322.5 metres tall and has 78 floors.

Engineers and architects design and construct skyscrapers. Somewhere in the world, someone is trying to design and build even taller skyscrapers. While these buildings were the tallest in 2023, they may not stay that way for long.

Building	Location	Height	Floors	Completed
Burj Khalifa	Dubai, United Arab Emirates	828 metres	163	2010
Merdeka	Kuala Lumpur, Malaysia	679 metres	118	2023
Shanghai Tower	Shanghai, China	632 metres	128	2015
Makkah Royal Clock Tower	Mecca, Saudi Arabia	601 metres	120	2012
Ping An Finance Centre	Shenzhen, China	599 metres	115	2017
Lotte World Tower	Seoul, South Korea	555 metres	123	2017
One World Trade Centre	New York City, United States of America	541 metres	94	2014
Guangzhou CTF Finance Centre	Guangzhou, China	530 metres	111	2016
Tianjin CTF Finance Centre	Tianjin, China	530 metres	97	2019
CITIC Tower	Beijing, China	538 metres	109	2018

TARGETING ENGLISH HOMEWORK YEAR 4 © PASCAL PRESS ISBN 978 1 925726 61 9

Reading & Comprehension

Shade the bubble next to the correct answer. Write the answer on the line where appropriate.

1. When was the information in this table correct?
   - ◯ 2023
   - ◯ today
   - ◯ forever

2. What is the purpose of the table?
   - ◯ to list tall buildings
   - ◯ to compare the tallest buildings in the world
   - ◯ to encourage people to build taller buildings

3. What information does the table provide? (Choose any that apply.)
   - ◯ the height of the buildings
   - ◯ the number of floors in the buildings
   - ◯ what the buildings are made of
   - ◯ where the buildings are located
   - ◯ when the buildings were completed

4. Where was the world's tallest building in 2023?
   - ◯ Dubai
   - ◯ Malaysia
   - ◯ China

5. Of the world's ten tallest buildings, how many are in **China**?
   - ◯ ten
   - ◯ seven
   - ◯ five

6. Which of these buildings is **not** in China?
   - ◯ Makkah Royal Clock Tower
   - ◯ Guangzhou CTF Finance Centre
   - ◯ CITIC Tower

7. Of the world's ten tallest buildings, which was the **first** to be completed?

   ____

   ____

8. Of the world's ten tallest buildings, which was the **last** to be completed?

   ____

   ____

9. What and where is Australia's tallest building?

   ____

   ____

10. Do you think these ten buildings will remain the tallest in the future?

    Explain: ______________________________

    ____

    ____

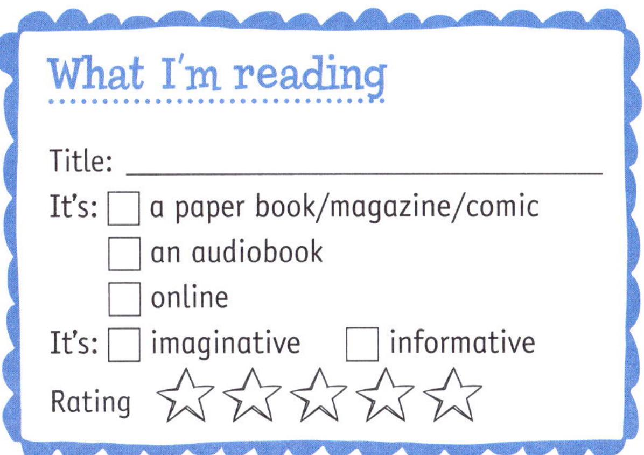

What I'm reading

Title: ______________________________

It's: ☐ a paper book/magazine/comic
☐ an audiobook
☐ online

It's: ☐ imaginative ☐ informative

Rating ☆☆☆☆☆

Score 2 points for each correct answer! SCORE /20

Grammar & Punctuation

TERM 1

AC9E4LA06, AC9E4LY06

Adjectives

Adjectives are words used to describe people, places and things. They work with a noun to tell us more about it. They help the reader to build up a clear picture of what is being described.

Adjectives can describe colour (green), size (short), shape (round), number (four), sound (loud), feelings (angry), qualities (mean).

Example: The **tall** buildings need to be **strong** and **stable**.

Read the sentences. Underline the adjectives. Circle the nouns that are being described.

1. In 2023, the world's tallest building was in the United Arab Emirates.
2. The Q1 building on the Gold Coast has 78 floors.
3. The Merdeka is 679 metres tall.
4. Skyscrapers must be able to hold an enormous amount of weight.
5. The world's tallest building is over 500 metres taller than the tallest building in Australia.

Comparative adjectives

Adjectives can be used to show how people or things compare to each other.

When two things are compared, you add the suffix **-er**.

Example: Australia's Q1 building is **tall**, but the One World Trade Centre is **taller**.

When more than two things are compared, you add the suffix **-est**.

Example: The Burj Khalifa is the **tallest** of all.

These comparative adjectives are tricky:

good – better – best

bad – worse – worst

many – more – most

little – less – least

Add the suffixes -er and -est to these adjectives.

	-er	-est
6. tall	________	________
7. short	________	________
8. high	________	________
9. safe	________	________
10. strong	________	________

Write the correct comparative adjective to complete each sentence.

11. A giraffe is ________ than a leopard. (tall)
12. A plane is ________ than a bird. (big)
13. A rocket flies ________ than a kite. (high)
14. An elephant is ________ than I am. (strong)
15. The Burj Khalifa is the ________ building in the world. (tall)

Use the word taller or shorter to complete these sentences.

16. The Lotte World Tower is ________ than the Shanghai Tower.
17. The Q1 building is ________ than the One World Trade Centre.
18. The CITIC Tower is ________ than Australia's tallest building.
19. The Guangzhou CTF Finance Centre is ________ than Makkah Royal Clock Tower.
20. The Ping An Finance Center is ________ than the Merdeka.

Score 2 points for each correct answer! SCORE /40    

TARGETING ENGLISH HOMEWORK YEAR 4 © PASCAL PRESS ISBN 978 1 925726 61 9

Phonic & Word Knowledge

AC9E4LY09, AC9E4LY10

Syllables

Syllables are chunks of sounds in words. We can tell how many chunks of sounds, or syllables, there are in a word by clapping the beats. Words may have 1, 2, 3 or even more syllables. We can also tell the number of syllables by counting the vowel sounds we hear. Each syllable has one vowel sound.

Read these words. Circle the vowel sounds. Remember: some vowels are spelt with two letters. Clap the syllables. Write the number of syllables on the line.

1. designers ________
2. knowledge ________
3. safely ________
4. stable ________
5. enormous ________
6. engineering ________
7. buildings ________
8. strong ________
9. tall ________
10. amount ________

Consonants

Breaking words into syllables is easy when you know how. It can even help you when you are reading words from other languages.

Double consonants: If the word has double consonants, you break between the consonants. *Example:* Makkah = Mak + kah

Two or more consonants: As for double consonants, you break between the consonants.

Example: Lumpur = Lum + pur

However, you do not break between the letters of a digraph or a blend.

Example: construct = con + struct

Read the words. Circle the vowel sounds. Show how to break the words into syllables.

11. Shanghai = __________ + __________
12. complete = __________ + __________
13. Guangzhou = __________ + __________
14. centre = __________ + __________
15. Shenzhen = __________ + __________
16. Mecca = __________ + __________
17. Makkah = __________ + __________
18. bubble = __________ + __________

Vowels

Sometimes a syllable may end or start with a vowel. Usually, we break before the consonant if the vowel sound is long. If the vowel sound is short, we usually break after the consonant.

Examples: China = Chi + na (the first syllable has a long vowel sound)
seven = sev + en (the first syllable has a short vowel sound)

Read the words. Circle the vowel sounds. Show how to break them into syllables.

19. design = __________ + __________
20. Dubai = __________ + __________
21. scrapers = __________ + __________
22. metres = __________ + __________
23. Asia = __________ + __________
24. Beijing = __________ + __________

More than two syllables

We use the same rules when we break longer words into syllables. Find the vowels first to find the number of syllables. Then look at the consonants to see where to make the breaks. Some longer words contain different kinds of breaks.

Examples: designer = de + sign + er
Khalifa = Kha + li + fa

Read the words. Circle the vowel sounds. Show how to break them into syllables.

25. enormous = _____ + _____ + _____
26. engineer = _____ + _____ + _____
27. united = _____ + _____ + _____
28. Malaysia = _____ + _____ + _____
29. Emirates = _____ + _____ + _____
30. Australia = _____ + _____ + _____ + _____

Score 2 points for each correct answer! SCORE /60 0-28 30-54 56-60

Reading & Comprehension

AC9E4LA03, AC9E4LA10, AC9E4LY03, AC9E4LY04, AC9E4LY05, AC9S4U01

Informative text – Report

Dung Beetles

Some people have clean jobs. Some people have dirty jobs. It's the same for animals.

The dung beetle has a dirty job. Its job is to collect the dung that cows and horses leave behind. Dung beetles work through the day and night, trying to clear away the dung. They drag it down under the ground, piece by piece.

Dung beetles lay their eggs in the dung to make more dung beetles. That way they can clear away even more dung.

Without the beetles to clear away the dung, the animals wouldn't be able to walk anywhere without stepping in it. Flies would lay their eggs in it. Maggots would hatch out of the eggs, and soon there'd be even more flies. Plants grow better and the air smells cleaner when dung beetles do their job.

Even though dung beetles are small, they do a job that no one else wants to do. Without dung beetles, the world wouldn't be a very pleasant place.

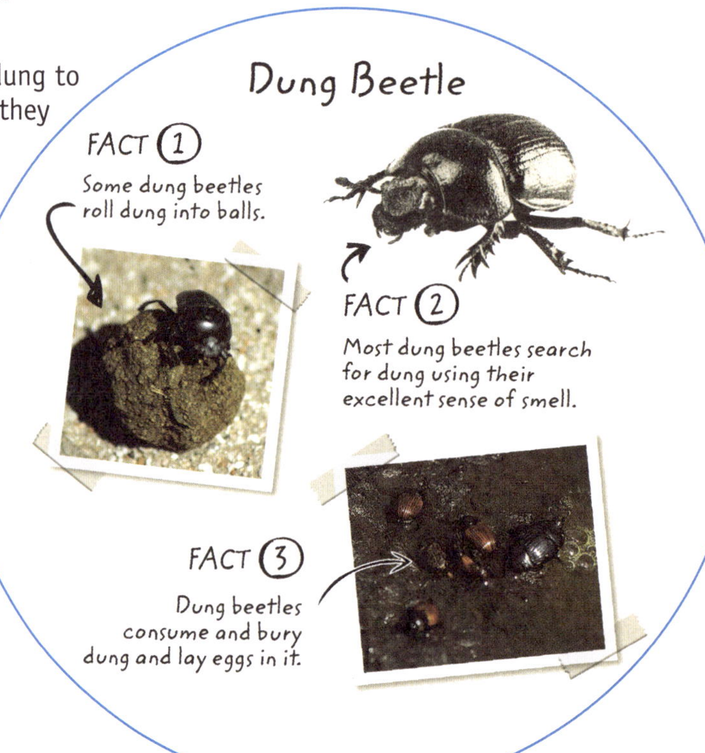

Source: Text and image adapted from *Doug the Dung Beetle* by Rebecca Johnson, Pascal Press.

TARGETING ENGLISH HOMEWORK YEAR 4 © PASCAL PRESS ISBN 978 1 925726 61 9

Reading & Comprehension

TERM 1

Shade the bubble next to the correct answer. Write the answer on the line where appropriate.

1. **Why are these beetles called dung beetles?**
   - ◯ because they smell bad
   - ◯ because they look like a ball of dung
   - ◯ because they clear away dung

2. **What do dung beetles do with the dung? (Choose any that apply.)**
   - ◯ drag it under the ground
   - ◯ lay their eggs in it
   - ◯ eat it

3. **Do all dung beetles roll dung into balls?**
   - ◯ Yes
   - ◯ No
   - ◯ Unsure

4. **Why do these beetles lay eggs in the dung?**
   - ◯ to make more dung beetles
   - ◯ because they don't want to make a nest
   - ◯ because the hospitals are too far away

5. **Which sense do most dung beetles use to find more dung?**
   - ◯ taste
   - ◯ touch
   - ◯ hearing
   - ◯ smell
   - ◯ sight

6. **What would happen if dung beetles didn't do their job? (Choose any that apply.)**
   - ◯ Animal poo wouldn't get cleared away.
   - ◯ There would be a lot of flies.
   - ◯ The world would be dirty and smelly.
   - ◯ Plants would grow better.

7. **What are the young of flies called?**
   - ◯ dung beetles
   - ◯ maggots
   - ◯ baby flies

8. **In what ways are dung beetles important? (Choose any that apply.)**
   - ◯ They clear away animal poo.
   - ◯ They attract flies.
   - ◯ They help the plants grow.
   - ◯ They make the air smell cleaner.

9. **How big do you think dung beetles might be?**
   - ◯ 3 cm
   - ◯ 30 cm
   - ◯ 300 cm

10. **Have you ever seen a dung beetle?**

    ____

    Where do you think would be the best place to look for a dung beetle?

    ____

    ____

Score 2 points for each correct answer! SCORE /20 0-8 10-14 16-20

Grammar & Punctuation

AC9E4LA08, AC9E4LY06

TERM 1

Verbs

Every sentence has a verb. Verbs are words that tell us what is happening in a sentence. They tell us what the subject of the sentence is doing, thinking, saying or feeling.

Example: Dung beetles **lay** their eggs in the dung.

Relating verbs help to link information in a sentence. They include verbs like am, is, are, were, was, have, has.

Example: The dung beetle **has** a dirty job. Dung beetles **are** small.

Underline the subject of each sentence. Circle the verb. Write D for a doing verb, R for a relating verb.

1. _____ Some people have clean jobs.
2. _____ Dung beetles collect dung left by cows and horses.
3. _____ Dung beetles work day and night.
4. _____ They drag it down under the ground, piece by piece.
5. _____ The world is a cleaner place with dung beetles in it.

Adverbs

Adverbs tell us more about verbs. They tell us **how** something is happening.

Example: Dung beetles work **hard**.

They tell us when, how often, how long or where things are happening.

Example: Dung beetles **always** work hard. Dung beetles clear dung **away**.

Circle the verb in each sentence. Underline the adverb. Write what the adverb tells about the verb: H (how), T (time/when), P (place/where).

6. _____ Animals couldn't walk anywhere.
7. _____ Maggots soon hatch.
8. _____ Plants grow better.
9. _____ Air smells cleaner.
10. _____ Dung beetles carry dung underground.

Adverbial phrases and prepositions

Adverbial phrases tell how, where, when and why things happen.

Examples:

Dung beetles work through the day and night. (when)

They drag it down under the ground. (where)

Adverbial phrases often begin with a preposition.

Examples of prepositions: about, above, across, after, almost, at, before, behind, below, by, down, during, except, for, from, in, into, near, of, off, on, over, past, since, through, till, to, under, until, up, upon, with

Underline the adverbial phrase in each sentence. Circle the preposition. Write what the adverbial phrase tells about the verb: H (how), T (time/when), P (place/where).

11. _____ Dung beetles lay their eggs in the dung.
12. _____ The beetles find dung with their sense of smell.
13. _____ Some dung beetles roll dung into balls.
14. _____ Maggots hatch out of eggs.
15. _____ Flies are a pest from morning till night.

Score 2 points for each correct answer! SCORE /30    

0-12 14-24 26-30

TARGETING ENGLISH HOMEWORK YEAR 4 © PASCAL PRESS ISBN 978 1 925726 61 9

Phonic & Word Knowledge

UNIT 6

AC9E4LY09, AC9E4LY11

TERM 1

Letter teams that make the long 'e' sound

Say each word from the word bank. Each word has the long 'e' sound. Underline the letters that spell the long 'e' sound.

beetles work fly has day hatch the
egg away best ground for very more
dung have some night under else
through not right same out that leave

Choose words from the word bank to complete these sentences.

1. Dung __________ are small but they do a big job.
2. Dung beetles carry the dung underground __________ by __________.
3. Some __________ do clean jobs and some people do dirty jobs.
4. Dung beetles collect the dung that horses and cows leave __________.
5. The world would be __________ dirty if dung beetles didn't do their job.

Syllables

Use the rules you know to show how to break these words into syllables.

6. beetle = __________ + __________
7. better = __________ + __________
8. people = __________ + __________
9. behind = __________ + __________
10. under = __________ + __________
11. collect = __________ + __________
12. maggots = __________ + __________
13. dirty = __________ + __________
14. stepping = __________ + __________
15. even = __________ + __________

Homophones

Homophones are words that sound the same but have a different spelling and meaning.

Circle the correct homophone in each sentence.

16. I read (some, sum) information about dung beetles.
17. Dung beetles lay (there, their) eggs in the dung left by cows and horses.
18. Dung beetles take the dung underground a (piece, peace) at a time.
19. Dung beetles do a great job (four, for) the world.
20. The (weigh, way) dung beetles work is amazing.
21. Dung beetles work (threw, through) the day and night.
22. No (one, won) else wants to do the dirty job that dung beetles do.
23. (Its, It's) a dirty job that dung beetles do.
24. Their job is (to, two, too) collect dung.

High-frequency words

High-frequency words occur frequently in text. It is good to memorise them so you recognise them by sight.

Word search. Circle these high-frequency words in the grid. Mark them off as you go.

has have some more that
night day leave work away
under egg ground same
through dung for hatch
right beetles else very the
best not out fly

H	A	S	D	W	U	N	D	E	R
A	F	O	R	O	L	I	U	G	I
V	L	M	O	R	E	G	N	G	G
E	Y	E	G	K	A	H	T	D	H
A	W	A	Y	B	U	T	H	A	T
E	V	S	A	M	E	E	R	Y	T
B	E	E	T	L	E	S	O	U	T
E	R	L	H	G	R	O	U	N	D
S	Y	S	E	D	U	N	G	O	L
T	E	E	H	A	T	C	H	T	S

25. When you have found all the words, the remaining letters, from left to right and top to bottom, will spell out a phrase. Write it here.

____

____

Score 2 points for each correct answer! SCORE /50

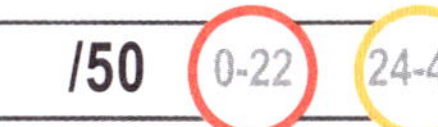

Imaginative text – Science Fiction

TERM 1

The Silver Ball of Hope (Part 1)

This story is an excerpt from *The Silver Ball of Hope*, Book 2 in the *Star Quest series* by Del Merrick. Read other chapters in the story in Units 15, 23 and 31.

The story so far: Tor and Cassini have been sent on a mission to Mylos to help save their home planet. Tor's little brother Cha hid in their spaceship, the 'Tarvos', and arrives on Mylos with them. Neither Tor nor Cassini are pleased to see him. During the landing, the spaceship is damaged.

While Cha sleeps soundly in his sleep capsule, Tor and Cassini work to fix the Tarvos.

Tor clicks a button on the communicator band on his wrist. King Padu's face appears on the small screen. Cassini looks over Tor's shoulder as they listen to the king's message.

"Lak-tor, your mission is to find the silver ball of hope. We know that it is hidden in Vulcha's lair deep in the Gravalon Crater. It will be well guarded. Be careful."

Tor looks at Cassini. "We may have to fight for the silver ball, Cassi."

"Then we'd better arm ourselves well," says Cassini.

Tor and Cassini gather up their neon rods and P16 sonic pulsators. Cassini ties a pouch filled with plasma bolts around her waist. Tor slips a dagger into his scabbard.

Cha pops his head out of his sleep capsule.

"Salu, Cass," he says cheerfully.

"Don't you salu me, Cha," Cassini says irritably. "You nearly made us crash yesterday."

Source: Image from and text adapted from *The Silver Ball of Hope*, the second book in the Star Quest series by Del Merrick, Blake Education.

TARGETING ENGLISH HOMEWORK YEAR 4 © PASCAL PRESS ISBN 978 1 925726 61 9

Reading & Comprehension

Use these clues to complete the crossword.

Across

3. The spaceship is named __________.
6. They were to find the __________ ball.
7. Tor's little brother __________ hid in the spaceship.
8. They travelled to Mylos in a __________.
12. Tor had a communicator band on his __________.
13. Cassini had a __________ tied to her waist.
14. The silver ball was in __________ Crater.

Down

1. Tor and __________ were sent to Mylos.
2. Tor and Cassini were sent to __________.
3. Cha is __________'s little brother.
4. They had to get the ball from __________.
5. Cassini had __________ bolts in a pouch.
9. The silver ball was hidden in a __________.
10. Tor got a message from King __________.
11. Cassini blamed Cha for the __________.

TERM 1

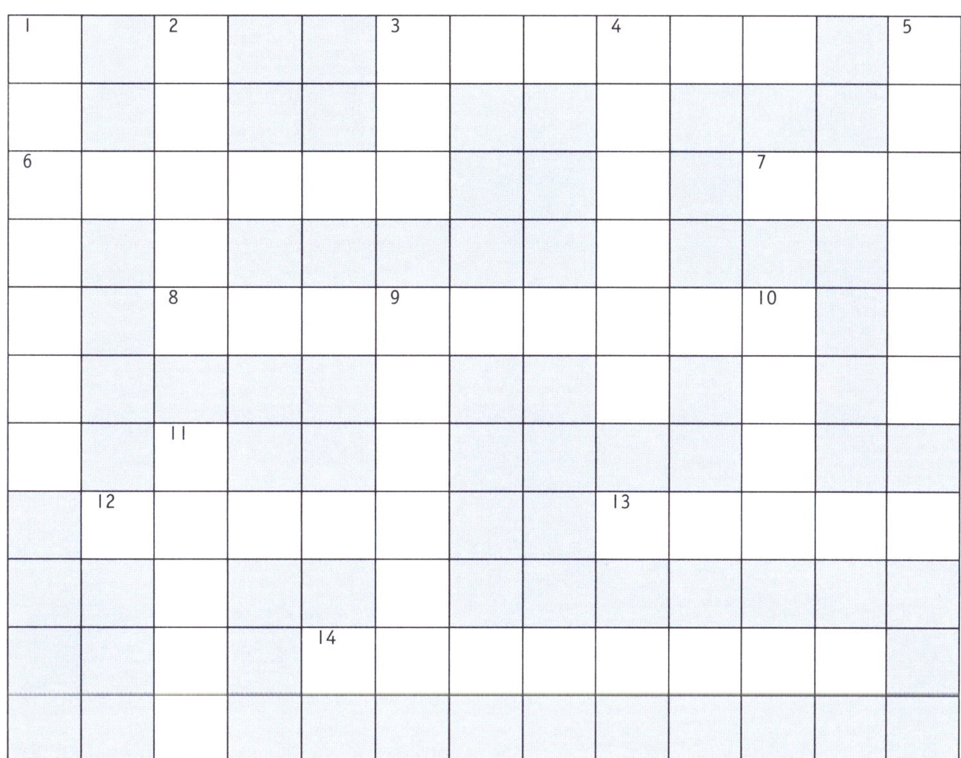

What I'm reading

Title: ____________________

It's: ☐ a paper book/magazine/comic
☐ an audiobook
☐ online

It's: ☐ imaginative ☐ informative

Rating ☆☆☆☆☆

Score 2 points for each correct answer! SCORE /30 0-12 14-24 26-30

Grammar & Punctuation

TERM 1

AC9E4LA04, AC9E4LA09, AC9E4LY06

Verb groups

A verb group has more than one verb. It is made up of a main verb and a helper verb.

Example: Tor and Cassini **are** going to Mylos.

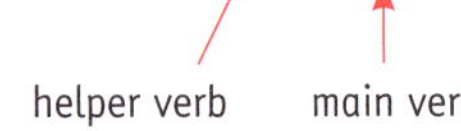

The helper verb is called an auxiliary verb.

Helper verbs include: am, is, are, was, were, be, being, been, do, does, did, has, have, had, will, shall.

Underline the verb group in these sentences.

1. Cha was hiding in their spaceship.
2. Tor and Cassini have been sent to Mylos.
3. Tor and Cassini will find the silver ball of hope.
4. They may have to fight for the silver ball.
5. The king is talking through a communicator on Tor's wrist.

Auxiliary verbs

Some auxiliary (helper) verbs tell us about time – whether things are happening in the present, the past or the future.

Examples:

Cha **is** sleeping in his space capsule. (present)

Cha **was** sleeping in his space capsule. (past)

Cha **will** sleep in his space capsule. (future)

Underline the verb group in these sentences. Write N if it is happening in the present or now, write P if it is happening in the past, write F if it will happen in the future.

6. _____ Tor and Cassini have been sent on a mission to Mylos.
7. _____ Neither Tor nor Cassini are pleased with Cha.
8. _____ Cassini was looking over Tor's shoulder at the king.
9. _____ They may have to fight for the silver ball.
10. _____ They will need to arm themselves.

Complete these sentences to show something happening in the present (N), past (P) or future (F). Use the main verb shown and an auxiliary verb.

11. (N) Tor _____________________ the damaged spaceship. (fix)
12. (P) Tor and Cassini _____________________ to Mylos. (sent)
13. (F) Cha _____________________ in the spaceship while Tor and Cassini search. (stay)
14. (P) Tor _____________________ to King Padu on his communicator band. (talk)
15. (F) Tor and Cassini _____________________ the silver ball of hope. (find)

Personal pronouns

Pronouns take the place of nouns. Personal pronouns replace the names of people, places, animals and things. We use pronouns so we don't have to repeat the same nouns over again.

Example: Cha hid in the spaceship. **He** was not supposed to be there.

Pronouns must agree with the nouns they replace in number and gender. Gender refers to male, female or neutral (it).

Singular: I, he, she, it, him, her, me, you

Plural: we, us, you, they, them

Circle the pronouns in these sentences. Underline the noun or nouns they replace.

16. Tor was working on the Tarvos because it was damaged.
17. Cassini looks over Tor's shoulder as they listen to the king's message.
18. The silver ball of hope was hidden, and it was well guarded.
19. Cassini looked at the dagger that Tor gave to her.
20. Cha was sleeping because he was tired.

Score 2 points for each correct answer!

SCORE /40

 ISBN 978 1 925726 61 9

AC9E4LY09, AC9E4LY10

The letter 'g'

We usually think of the letter 'g' representing the 'hard g' sound, as in goat and guard.

When the letter 'g' is followed by the vowels 'e', 'i' or 'y', it makes the sound 'j' like in jam and is called the 'soft g' sound.

Examples: gem   wage

It also combines with the letter 'n' to make the digraph 'ng', as in ring.

When it comes before the letter 'n' to make the digraph 'gn', it is silent, as in gnome.

Read the words. Circle the letter 'g'. Write H for 'hard g', J for 'soft g', NG for the digraph 'ng' and S if the letter 'g' is silent.

1. _____ sign
2. _____ sing
3. _____ Gravalon
4. _____ guard
5. _____ during
6. _____ damage
7. _____ gnat
8. _____ gem
9. _____ landing
10. _____ dagger

Word origins

The word excerpt comes from a Latin word 'excarpere' which means 'plucked out'.

An excerpt is a part of a book or a piece of music that has been selected or taken out.

The prefix 'ex-' means 'out'. It usually comes before a vowel or the consonants 't' and 'c'.

Examples: exit   extract   exceed

The letter 'e-' is a variant of the prefix 'ex-'. It usually comes before a consonant.

Examples: emit   eject   emigrate

We have many other words that begin with the prefix 'ex-' or its variant 'e-'.

Draw lines to match the words to their meanings.

11. exit	to take out or remove
12. extend	to go beyond expectations
13. exceed	the way out
14. exclude	a passage taken out of a book
15. extract	to throw out
16. excerpt	to stretch out
17. emit	to send out, e.g. light
18. eject	to breathe out
19. emigrate	to shut out
20. exhale	to move out of a country

Syllables

Say the words in the word bank. Clap the syllables. Sort the words into the table.

silver	quest	Gravalon	mission
planet	Cassini	pulsators	spaceship
waist	brother	hope	yesterday
crash	sleep	communicator	

1 syllable
21.
22.
23.
24.
25.
2 syllables
26.
27.
28.
29.
30.
3+ syllables
31.
32.
33.
34.
35.

Score 2 points for each correct answer!

SCORE /70

Book review: *The Golden Llama*

The Golden Llama (League of Llamas, Book 1)

Reviewed by Olivia, 10, Victoria

The Golden Llama by Aleesah Darlison, with illustrations by Simon Greiner, Puffin Books, ISBN: 9781760894160

I really enjoyed this book. It is hilarious. There are so many funny word plays and puns that made me laugh out loud.

There are four League of Llama books. *The Golden Llama* is the first one in the series. They are chapter books, but they have illustrations so younger kids can read them too.

The League of Llamas (LOL) are spies whose mission is to save the world from their arch-enemy General Bottomburp. In *The Golden Llama*, General Bottomburp and his evil beavers have stolen the Golden Llama statue. The LOL have to get it back.

I think younger kids would just enjoy the story, but older kids like me would get the jokes. Even my parents like to read bits out loud. They say the top spy Phillipe Llamar, otherwise known as 0011, is like James Bond 007.

I like the way the Llamas' names are spelt with double ll, like Phillipe, Lloyd and Elloise. Lots of other words are spelt with double ll too, like llamaborghinis and prob-llama (as in 'no prob-llama'). Mama Llamas' name rhymes, and General Bottomburp (which is hilarious) has alliteration too. I thought President Ollama was really funny, but I don't think little kids would know who he is.

There is so much in *The Golden Llama* to enjoy.

I recommend it for readers over 7, especially older readers who like a good laugh.

I give it 5 stars.

TARGETING ENGLISH HOMEWORK YEAR 4 © PASCAL PRESS ISBN 978 1 925726 61 9

Review

Shade the bubble next to the correct answer. Write the answer on the line where appropriate.

1. Do you think you'd like to read *The Golden Llama*?
   - ◯ Yes
   - ◯ No
   - ◯ Unsure

2. Which words or phrases in the review help you decide?

____
____
____
____
____
____

3. List some books that you have read during the term.

____
____
____
____
____
____

4. Circle your favourite.

Now you can write a review of your favourite book so that others can decide whether to read it or not.

1. About the book.

Title: ______________________________
Author: ______________________________
Illustrator: ______________________________
Publisher: ______________________________
ISBN: ______________________________

2. Circle the word that best describes the type of story.

science fiction fantasy fairy tale
realistic fiction historical fiction
adventure mystery poetry
fable humour comic picture book

If the type of story is not listed, write it here: ______________________________

The characters

3. Who is the main character (MC)?

Name: ______________________________
Age: ______________________________
Country of birth: ______________________________
Physical features: ______________________________
____
____

Personality: ______________________________
____
____

Likes: ______________________________
____
____
____

Dislikes: ______________________________
____
____
____

Goal (what the character wants to achieve):
____
____
____
____
____
____

4. Who are the supporting characters?

Names: ______________________________
____
____
____
____
____
____

Specialities (what they are good at):
____
____
____
____
____
____

TERM 1

TERM 1

How they support (help) the MC:

⑤ **Who are the villains or baddies?**

Names:

Specialities (what they are good at):

How they try to foil (stop) the MC:

The setting

⑥ **Where is the story set? Where and when does the story take place?**

The plot

⑦ **What happens in the beginning of the story?**

Complication

⑧ **What happens that makes a problem for the characters?**

⑨ **How do they try to solve the problem?**

First:

Second:

Third:

⑩ **Is the problem solved?**

◯ Yes
◯ No
◯ Unsure

TARGETING ENGLISH HOMEWORK YEAR 4 © PASCAL PRESS ISBN 978 1 925726 61 9

Review

Conclusion

11. What happens at the end of the story? How do things work out for the characters?

12. What is your favourite part of the story?

Why?

Draw your favourite part.

13. Who else would like to read this book? Who do you recommend it for?

14. How many stars do you give it?

TARGETING ENGLISH HOMEWORK YEAR 4 © PASCAL PRESS ISBN 978 1 925726 61 9

Reading & Comprehension

Birdy Street

My heart was beating faster as I strapped on my freshly painted Zipper helmet and squeezed into the seat.

Nick and Owen gave me a push and I was off. I got faster and faster as I went downhill.

I looked back. Nick and Owen were following me on their skateboards, but they were zigzagging.

I tried to zigzag too by pulling on the steering rope that was attached to the front axle. Yikes! I nearly swerved out of control, into a pole.

"Help me, you guys!" I shouted. "No brakes!" But Nick and Owen had already hopped off their skateboards and were left far behind.

Soon I was going very fast.

"Yeeearrgh!!!!" I screamed as I sped, out of control, down the steepest part of the hill.

Source: Text adapted from *The Zipper* by David Dickson, Sparklers, Blake Education.

Shade the bubble next to the correct answer. Write the answer on the line where appropriate.

1. **Why was Nathan's heart beating faster?**
   - ◯ He was excited.
   - ◯ He was nervous.
   - ◯ He had been running.

2. **Who gave Nathan a push in the billycart?**
   - ◯ Neil and Owen
   - ◯ Nick and Owen
   - ◯ Owen and Dad

3. **How did Owen and Nick go down the hill?**
   - ◯ in a billycart
   - ◯ on their skateboards
   - ◯ on their bikes

4. **Why were Own and Nick zigzagging?**
   - ◯ to go faster
   - ◯ to go slower
   - ◯ to hide from Nathan

5. **How did Nathan steer the Zipper?**
   - ◯ with a rope tied to the front axle
   - ◯ with a rope tied to the back axle
   - ◯ with a steering wheel

6. **Was it a good way of steering the billycart?**
   ◯ Yes ◯ No ◯ Unsure

7. **Explain:** ______________________________

   ____

   ____

   ____

8. **What problems did Nathan have with the Zipper billycart? (Choose any that apply.)**
   - ◯ He couldn't steer it.
   - ◯ It had no brakes.
   - ◯ He didn't know how to stop it.

9. **Why do you think Nick and Owen got off their skateboards?**

   ____

   ____

   ____

   ____

10. **What do you think will happen now?**

   ____

   ____

   ____

   ____

Score 2 points for each correct answer! SCORE /20 0-8 10-14 16-20

TARGETING ENGLISH HOMEWORK YEAR 4 © PASCAL PRESS ISBN 978 1 925726 61 9

Grammar & Punctuation

TERM 1

Sentences

Punctuate these sentences correctly using **capital letters, full stops, questions marks** and **exclamation marks**. Write **S** for statement, **Q** for question, **C** for command, **E** for exclamation.

1. _____ help the billycart is out of control
2. _____ how can you make a marshmallow fly
3. _____ did you know that nosebleeds are a sign of alien abduction
4. _____ this is the best book I've ever read
5. _____ cut the bottom out of the yoghurt cup
6. _____ the Burj Khalifa is the tallest building in the world
7. _____ place the marshmallow inside the yoghurt cup
8. _____ dung beetles make the world a cleaner place
9. _____ who wrote The Golden Llama
10. _____ stop thief

Underline the **subject**, circle the **verb** and highlight the **object** in these sentences.

11. Tor and Cassini repaired the damaged spaceship.
12. Nathan rode The Zipper down Birdy Street.
13. Lara shot a marshmallow out of a popper.
14. Dung beetles clean up animal poo.
15. Aliens abducted Hamish.

Rewrite each of these commands as a **statement** to tell what you did in this gravity experiment. Each statement will begin with 'I' and use past tense.

16. Line up the ball, rock and feather at the edge of the table.

____

____

17. Use the ruler to push the objects off the table at the same time.

____

____

18. Watch what object hits the floor first.

____

____

19. Record the order in which the objects hit the floor.

____

____

20. Repeat the experiment to be sure of your results.

____

____

Nouns

Sort these **nouns** into the table below.

worry beetle Nathan Runt
fear Burj Khalifa spaceship
idea communication Mylos
marshmallow hope building
Australia billycart

Common nouns
21
22
23
24
25

Abstract nouns
26
27
28
29
30

Proper nouns
31
32
33
34
35

Direct speech

Underline the **words spoken** in these sentences. Circle the **saying verb**. Highlight **the name of the character** who says them.

36. "You're not taking it to the tip, are you?" said Nathan.
37. "So, what are up to, Hamish?" asked Trev.
38. "Lak-tor, your mission is to find the silver ball of hope," commanded King Padu.
39. "The Burj Khalifa is the world's tallest building," Noah boasted.
40. "I think I've been abducted by aliens," whimpered Hamish.

Grammar & Punctuation

Noun groups

Add words to these nouns to form noun groups.

41 spaceship ____________________

42 alien ____________________

43 billycart ____________________

44 marshmallow ____________________

45 building ____________________

Comparative adjectives

Write the correct comparative adjective to complete each sentence.

46 The billycart was going down the hill ____________ and ____________. (fast)

47 Tor's brother is ____________ than him. (young)

48 Australia's ____________ building is on the Gold Coast. (tall)

49 Dung beetles help to make our world ____________. (clean)

50 My marshmallow popper is the ____________ in the class. (good)

Adverbial phrases

Underline the adverbial phrase in each sentence. Circle the preposition. Write what the adverbial phrase tells about the verb: H (how), T (time/when), P (place/where).

51 _____ Annie Shearer lives on a sheep farm.

52 _____ Nathan helped his father sort junk on Saturday.

53 _____ Place the marshmallow in the cup.

54 _____ Cut the paper with care.

55 _____ Run away from the aliens very fast.

Score 2 points for each correct answer!

SCORE /110 0-52 54-104 106-110

Phonic & Word Knowledge

Vowel sounds

Say each word. Some have short vowel sounds. Some have long vowel sounds. Be careful – there are different ways of spelling the vowel sounds.

Dad	give	help	peace	was
home	junk	cube	heavy	stack
frame	paint	ride	zip	some
rope	said	nick	drag	day
keep	pie	off	stuff	huge
road	fly	piece	new	lot

Sort the words into the table.

Short 'a'	Short 'e'
1	4
2	5
3	6
Short 'i'	**Short 'o'**
7	10
8	11
9	12
Short 'u'	**Long 'a'**
13	16
14	17
15	18
Long 'e'	**Long 'i'**
19	22
20	23
21	24
Long 'o'	**Long 'u'**
25	28
26	29
27	30

TARGETING ENGLISH HOMEWORK YEAR 4 © PASCAL PRESS ISBN 978 1 925726 61 9

Phonic & Word Knowledge

TERM 1

Verb tense

Write the **past tense** and **present tense** forms of the base verbs. Be careful. We don't always add -ed to make the past tense. Some verbs are irregular.

	Base verb	Did (past tense)	Doing now (present tense)
31	knot		
32	cross		
33	tell		
34	drive		
35	write		
36	ride		
37	fall		
38	shop		
39	jump		
40	fly		

Contractions

Write a **contraction** for each pair of words.

41 you are ____________________
42 do not ____________________
43 was not ____________________
44 I have ____________________
45 should not ____________________
46 I would ____________________
47 could not ____________________
48 can not ____________________
49 we are ____________________
50 did not ____________________

Syllables

Say the words in the word bank. Clap the **syllables**. Sort the words into the following tables.

billycart	brakes	zipper
helmet	heart	marshmallow
farm	soon	Saturday
downhill	zigzagging	skateboard

	1 syllable
51	
52	
53	
54	
	2 syllables
55	
56	
57	
58	
	3+ syllables
59	
60	
61	
62	

Use the rules you know to show how to break these words into **syllables**.

63 zipper = __________ + __________
64 zigzag = __________ + __________
65 helmet = __________ + __________
66 exhale = __________ + __________
67 emit = __________ + __________
68 avoid = __________ + __________
69 before = __________ + __________
70 review = __________ + __________

Homophones

Circle the correct **homophone** in each sentence.

71 I ran (through, threw) the forest and over the bridge.

72 Runt was so fast and agile that he (one, won) the top prize in the dog show.

73 The teacher wrote (sum, some) problems on the board for us to solve.

74 The children didn't know (where, wear) the spaceship had come from.

75 The children thought the aliens had taken (their, there) books.

Score 2 points for each correct answer!

AC9E4LA03, AC9E4LY03, AC9E4LY04, AC9E4LY05

Imaginative text – Anecdote

TERM 2

Rodeo Riding

This is my news. On the weekend, my dad and I went to the rodeo in Mount Isa, and I went in the ring! I can show you a video that my dad took on his phone. The buck was pretty wild, but I managed to stay on for fifty-two seconds. I was pretty good for my age range, so I got this purple runner-up ribbon.

Dad was pretty stoked because he used to ride broncos when he was young. He reckoned I did pretty well for a ten-year-old, but Mum wasn't too pleased. We aren't talking about it, and she went and sat in the ute. So, it was a pretty awesome ride.

I was a little bit scared because I've fallen off a horse heaps before, but not in front of hundreds of people. I thought I would be embarrassed, but I wasn't because they all were cheering. So, I felt pretty cool, and I definitely want to be a cowboy when I grow up.

Source: Text adapted from *Rural School of the Air* by Sandie Eldridge, in Australian Readers' Theatre Middle Primary, Blake Education.

TARGETING ENGLISH HOMEWORK YEAR 4 © PASCAL PRESS ISBN 978 1 925726 61 9

Reading & Comprehension

Shade the bubble next to the correct answer. Write the answer on the line where appropriate.

1. Who do you think is telling the story?
   - ◯ a news reporter on television
   - ◯ a child at school
   - ◯ a child talking to their parents

2. When did the narrator go to the rodeo?
   - ◯ last week
   - ◯ during the holidays
   - ◯ on the weekend

3. Where was the rodeo?
   - ◯ in Mount Isa
   - ◯ at school
   - ◯ on the narrator's property

4. What did the narrator do at the rodeo?
   - ◯ had a hot dog
   - ◯ watched their dad ride a bronco
   - ◯ rode a horse

5. How long did the narrator stay on the horse?
   - ◯ two seconds
   - ◯ fifty-two seconds
   - ◯ fifty-two minutes

6. Did the narrator win the event?
   - ◯ Yes
   - ◯ No
   - ◯ Unsure

7. What colour ribbon did the narrator get?
   - ◯ red
   - ◯ blue
   - ◯ purple

8. How old is the narrator?
   - ◯ 10 years old
   - ◯ 12 years old
   - ◯ Unsure

9. Had the narrator ridden in a rodeo before?
   - ◯ Yes
   - ◯ No

   Explain: ______________________________

10. How did the narrator feel after their ride?
    - ◯ embarrassed
    - ◯ excited
    - ◯ scared

    Do you think the narrator is a boy or a girl?

    ____

    Explain: ______________________________

TERM 2

What I'm reading

Title: ______________________________

It's: ☐ a paper book/magazine/comic
☐ an audiobook
☐ online

It's: ☐ imaginative ☐ informative

Rating ☆ ☆ ☆ ☆ ☆

Score 2 points for each correct answer!

SCORE /20

Grammar & Punctuation

AC9E4LA06, AC9E4LA12

Simple sentences

Remember! A sentence is a group of words that makes sense on its own.

A simple sentence has one subject and one verb. It may also contain an object.

Circle the verb, underline the subject and highlight the object in each of these sentences.

1. I rode a horse in the rodeo.
2. The runner-up got a purple ribbon.
3. Dad took a video on his phone.
4. The people clapped their hands.
5. I wore my cowboy hat in the ring.

Clauses

A clause is a group of words with one subject and one verb. A simple sentence consists of one clause. It is an independent clause.

The subject and the verb must agree. That means a singular subject must have a singular verb, and a plural subject must have a plural verb.

Examples: **I am** going to the rodeo.
We are going to the rodeo.

Choose the correct verb to complete each sentence.

6. We ______________ been to the rodeo every year. (has/have)
7. She ______________ never been to the the rodeo. (has/have)
8. We ______________ photos with a camera. (take/takes)
9. Dad ______________ videos with his phone. (take/takes)
10. They ______________ to school in a bus but Sue ______________ in a car. (travel/travels)

Compound sentences

A compound sentence consists of two independent clauses, or two simple sentences joined together. Each clause makes sense on its own.

The two simple sentences are joined by a joining word, also called a conjunction.

Joining words include and, but, so, because, then and while.

We separate the two simple sentences by using a comma before the conjunction.

Example: My dad and I **went** to the rodeo in Mount Isa, and I **went** in the ring!

Both clauses could be written as separate sentences.

Example: My dad and I **went** to the rodeo in Mount Isa. I **went** in the ring!

Read these compound sentences. Circle the verbs, underline the subjects and highlight the conjunction or joining word.

11. The buck was pretty wild, but I managed to stay on for fifty-two seconds.
12. I was good for my age range, so I got this purple runner-up ribbon.
13. Dad was pretty stoked because he used to ride broncos.
14. Dad said I did well, but Mum wasn't too pleased.
15. I felt pretty cool, and I definitely want to be a cowboy.

Use a conjunction to join these simple sentences into a compound sentence.

16. I was a bit scared. I did my best.

____

____

17. Mum wasn't pleased. She sat in the car on her own.

____

____

Score 2 points for each correct answer! SCORE /34   

TERM 2

TARGETING ENGLISH HOMEWORK YEAR 4 © PASCAL PRESS ISBN 978 1 925726 61 9

AC9E4LY09, AC9E4LY10

Words that end with the long 'o' sound

Say each word from the word bank. Each word ends with the long 'o' sound. Underline the letters that spell the long 'o' sound.

show	grow	bronco	no
though	potato	so	slow
Joe	dough	plateau	volcano

Choose words from the box to complete these sentences.

1. I rode a ______________ on the weekend.
2. My friend ______________ came to the rodeo with me.
3. Joe didn't ride a bronco ______________.
4. After the ______________, we went out for pizza.
5. It was fun because we got to make our own pizza ______________.

Words that end with the long 'e' and long 'o' sound

Say each word from the word bank. Each word ends with the long 'e' and long 'o' sound. Each sound is a different syllable. Underline the letters that spell the two sounds.

rodeo	video	stereo	radio
studio	audio	polio	embryo
folio	scenario	Julio	cardio

Draw lines to match the words to their meanings.

6. rodeo	sound that comes through two or more speakers
7. radio	sound that people can hear
8. video	a horse-riding contest
9. stereo	a device for listening to news and music sent over radio waves
10. audio	a recording of moving visual images, often including sound

Syllables

Say the words in the word bank. Clap the syllables. Sort the words into the table.

phone	weekend	purple	video
embarrassed	horse	rodeo	range
bronco	buck	cheerfully	people

1 syllable
11
12
13
14
2 syllables
15
16
17
18
3+ syllables
19
20
21
22

Copy the words from 19 – 22. Show how to break them into syllables using the + sign.

23. ______________________
24. ______________________
25. ______________________
26. ______________________

Past tense of regular verbs

There are three ways of pronouncing the -ed ending of past tense verbs: t, d and id.

In verbs that end in a voiceless consonant like 'p', 'k', 's', 'ch' or 'sh', the '-ed' is pronounced t and does not form an extra syllable.

Examples: stopped, talked

In verbs that end with a vowel sound or a voiced consonant like 'b', 'm', 'v', or 'z', the '-ed' is pronounced d and does not form an extra syllable.

Examples: showed, robbed

In verbs that end with a 'd' or a 't', the '-ed' is pronounced id and forms an extra syllable.

Examples: wanted, needed

Read these words. Write t, d, or id for the sound made by the ending 'ed'.

27. batted _____
28. stoked _____
29. pleased _____
30. embarrassed _____
31. landed _____
32. videoed _____

Score 2 points for each correct answer! SCORE /64

TERM 2

Informative text – Report

Racing Boats on a River without Water

Have you ever heard of a boat race without water? There is such a thing. It is held on the dry sandy bed of the Todd River in Alice Springs, Central Australia. It is the only dry river boat race in the world. It is held every year on the third Saturday in August. It is called the *Todd River Race* and has been running for more than 60 years. People come from all over Australia, and even the world, for the fun event.

The boats are bottomless, just like the cars in the Flintstones cartoons. They may be made from a metal frame and covered in advertising banners. They may be old washtubs or bathtubs. They might look like yachts or canoes. The teams often dress up like pirates or Vikings or other seafarers. They stand inside their boats and carry them as they run along the riverbed.

The race can't be held if there is water in the river. In 1993, the river flooded, and the race was cancelled. It was cancelled again in 2020 because of the pandemic. In 60 years, there wasn't much that could stop this crazy boat race.

TARGETING ENGLISH HOMEWORK YEAR 4 © PASCAL PRESS ISBN 978 1 925726 61 9

Reading & Comprehension

Shade the bubble next to the correct answer. Write the answer on the line where appropriate.

1. What is different about this boat race?
   - ◯ There is no water in the river.
   - ◯ It is held once every 60 years.
   - ◯ It is held when the river floods.

2. Where is the race held?
   - ◯ in Alice Springs
   - ◯ in Sydney
   - ◯ in Hobart

3. When is the race held?
   - ◯ August
   - ◯ every third Saturday
   - ◯ once every 60 years

4. How many times has the race been cancelled?
   - ◯ once
   - ◯ twice
   - ◯ many times

5. Why was the race cancelled in 1993?
   - ◯ The river was flooded.
   - ◯ There was no water in the river.
   - ◯ There was a pandemic.

6. What is different about the boats?
   - ◯ They have no sails.
   - ◯ They have no bottoms.
   - ◯ They have wheels.

7. What are the boats made of? (Choose any that apply.)
   - ◯ cardboard cartons
   - ◯ metal frames
   - ◯ bathtubs

8. How do the boats move?
   - ◯ The wind and water carry them along.
   - ◯ They run on wheels.
   - ◯ People stand inside the boats and carry them.

9. What do the racing teams dress up as?
   - ◯ cowboys
   - ◯ emergency workers
   - ◯ pirates and Vikings

10. Why do you think people come from all over Australia and around the world to watch the boat race?

____

____

____

____

____

____

____

Would you like to watch the boat race?

____

Explain: ______________________________

____

____

____

____

____

____

TERM 2

What I'm reading

Title: ______________________________

It's: ☐ a paper book/magazine/comic
☐ an audiobook
☐ online

It's: ☐ imaginative ☐ informative

Rating ☆ ☆ ☆ ☆ ☆

Score 2 points for each correct answer!

SCORE /20 0-8 10-14 16-20

Grammar & Punctuation

AC9E4LA06

Sentences

A clause is a group of words with one subject and one verb.

A simple sentence consists of one clause. It is an independent clause.

A compound sentence is made up of two simple sentences. They are both independent clauses. They are joined by a conjunction.

Read these sentences. Circle the verbs and underline the subjects. Write S for a simple sentence and C for a compound sentence. Highlight the conjunction in any compound sentences.

1. _____ A boat race without water is held in Alice Springs every year.
2. _____ It is the only dry river boat race in the world.
3. _____They stand inside their boats, and they carry them along.
4. _____ In 1993 the river flooded, so the race was cancelled.
5. _____ They may be old washtubs or bathtubs.

Sometimes, if the clauses have the same subject, the subject is not repeated. It is understood.

Example: It is called the Todd River Race, and (it) has been running for more than 60 years. Sometimes the subject of each clause is different.

Example: It **is** the only boat race in the world, (so) people come from everywhere.

Use conjunctions to join these pairs of clauses into compound sentences.

6. The race is held in Alice Springs. It is held on the third Saturday in August.

____

____

7. People come from all over Australia. It is the only dry river race in the world.

____

____

8. The boats are bottomless. People carry them along.

____

____

9. Some people dress up like pirates. Some people dress up like Vikings.

____

____

10. The river flooded. The race was cancelled.

____

____

Adverbial phrases

Remember! Adverbial phrases tell us more about verbs. They tell us how, when, where or why things are done or are happening. Unlike a clause, a phrase doesn't make sense on its own. A phrase is a group of words that usually begins with a preposition.

Examples of prepositions:

at in until from between
on to under with near
for above

Underline the adverbial phrase in each sentence. Circle the preposition. Write what the adverbial phrase tells about the verb: H (how), T (time/when), P (place/where), W (why).

11. _____ The race is held on the dry sandy riverbed.
12. _____ It has been running for more than 60 years.
13. _____ People come from all over the world.
14. _____ They come to watch the race.
15. _____ They dress up like pirates.

Score 2 points for each correct answer!

TERM 2

TARGETING ENGLISH HOMEWORK YEAR 4 © PASCAL PRESS ISBN 978 1 925726 61 9

Phonic & Word Knowledge

AC9E4LY09, AC9E4LY10

TERM 2

Past tense of regular verbs

Say the words in the word bank. Underline the **'ed' ending**. Sort the words into the table according to the sound represented by 'ed'.

called	covered	demanded	looked
flooded	raced	painted	walked
carried	cancelled	dressed	waited

't'
(1)
(2)
(3)
(4)
'd'
(5)
(6)
(7)
(8)
'id'
(9)
(10)
(11)
(12)

Past tense of irregular verbs

Draw lines to match the **base verb** with its **past tense verb**.

(13) hear	came
(14) hold	made
(15) run	stood
(16) come	heard
(17) make	ran
(18) stand	held

Sounds of the letter 'a'

The letter 'a' is used to represent different sounds.
In sand, it has the 'short a' sound.
In race, it has the 'long a' sound.
In car, it works with 'r' to make the 'ar' sound.
In walk, it makes the 'or' sound.
In washtub, it makes the 'short o' sound.
In along, it makes the schwa or 'uh' sound.
There are other ways of spelling these sounds too.

Say the words in the word bank. Sort the words into the table according to the sound represented by **'a' on its own** or **in combination** with another letter.

call	cancel	race	bath	yacht
washtub	water	cartoons		pirates
crazy	canoe	about	may	sandy
central	was	all	can't	

short a	long a
(19)	(22)
(20)	(23)
(21)	(24)
ar	**or**
(25)	(28)
(26)	(29)
(27)	(30)
short o	**schwa**
(31)	(34)
(32)	(35)
(33)	(36)

The word **Australia** has **3 letter a's**. Each represents a different sound. Write the sound represented by each letter 'a'.

(37) Aus = _____ (38) tra = _____ (39) lia = _____

Schwa sound

Remember! Words with two or more syllables may have one or more unstressed syllables. The vowel in the unstressed syllable usually has the schwa sound 'uh'.

Break these words into **syllables**. Circle the unstressed syllable. Write the letter or letters that represent the **schwa sound**.

(40) river = ________ + ________ (_____)

(41) August = ________ + ________ (_____)

(42) central = ________ + ________ (_____)

(43) even = ________ + ________ (_____)

Score 2 points for each correct answer! SCORE /86

AC9E4LA03, AC9E4LY03, AC9E4LY04, AC9E4LY05, AC9E4LE03

Imaginative text – Poem

TERM 2

A Naughty Little Comet

by Ella Wheeler Wilcox

There was once a little comet who lived near the Milky Way!
She loved to wander out at night and jump about and play.
The mother of the comet was a very good old star -
She used to scold her reckless child for venturing out too far;
She told her of the ogre, Sun, who loved on stars to sup,
And who asked no better pastimes than gobbling comets up.

But instead of growing cautious and of showing proper fear,
The foolish little comet edged up near, and near, and near.
She switched her saucy tail along right where the Sun could see,
And flirted with old Mars and was bold as bold could be.
She laughed to scorn the quiet stars, who never frisked about;
She said there was no fun in life unless you ventured out.

She liked to make the planets stare, and wished no better mirth
Than just to see the telescopes aimed at her from the Earth.
She wondered how so many stars could mope through nights and days,
And let the sickly faced old moon get all the love and praise.
And as she talked and tossed her head and switched her shining trail,
The staid old mother star grew sad, her cheek grew wan and pale.

For she had lived there in the skies a million years or more,
And she had heard gay comets talk in just this way before.
And by and by there came an end to this gay comet's fun -
She went a tiny bit too far - and vanished in the Sun!
No more she swings her shining trail before the whole world's sight,
But quiet stars she laughed to scorn are twinkling every night.

TARGETING ENGLISH HOMEWORK YEAR 4 © PASCAL PRESS ISBN 978 1 925726 61 9

Reading & Comprehension

Write your answers on the lines provided.

1. What is the title of the poem?

2. Who wrote the poem?

3. Who or what is the poem about?

4. Where did the little comet live?

5. What did the little comet do that was naughty?

6. Who is the villain in the poem? Explain.

7. List the space objects that are mentioned in the poem.

8. Why did the mother star grow sad?

9. What happened to the little comet at the end?

10. What lesson do you think the poem is trying to teach?

TERM 2

What I'm reading

Title: ____________________

It's: ☐ a paper book/magazine/comic
☐ an audiobook
☐ online

It's: ☐ imaginative ☐ informative

Rating ☆☆☆☆☆

Score 2 points for each correct answer!

SCORE /20 0-8 10-14 16-20

TARGETING ENGLISH HOMEWORK YEAR 4 © PASCAL PRESS ISBN 978 1 925726 61 9

Grammar & Punctuation

AC9E4LA04, AC9E4LA06, AC9E4LE04

TERM 2

Word order

Most poems are written with a particular rhythm or beat. The rhythm is created by a pattern of stressed and unstressed syllables.

Sometimes in a poem, the order of words in sentences is changed so that the pattern of stressed and unstressed syllables, or the rhythm, as well as the rhyme, can be maintained.

Example: She told her of the ogre, Sun, who loved on stars to sup.

Usually, we would say: who loved to eat stars. ('sup' means to eat)

Read these sentences. Rewrite them as we would normally say or write them.

1. ... who asked no better pastimes than gobbling comets up.

____

____

2. She switched her saucy tail along right where the Sun could see.

____

____

3. No more she swings her shining trail before the whole world's sight.

____

____

Personal pronouns

Remember! Pronouns take the place of nouns. We use pronouns so we don't have to repeat the same nouns over again.

Example: There was once a little comet. **She** loved to wander out at night.

Pronouns must agree with the nouns they replace in number and gender.

Singular: I, he, she, it, him, her, me, you

Plural: we, us, you, they, them

'Who' is also a pronoun and is a placeholder for a person.

Example: There was once a little comet **who** lived near the Milky Way!

Circle the pronouns in these sentences. Write the noun they replace. You may need to look back at the poem.

4. She used to scold her reckless child for venturing out too far. ______________

5. The mother warned her of the ogre, Sun, who loved on stars to sup. ______________

6. She flirted with old Mars and was bold as bold could be. ______________

7. The little comet laughed to scorn the quiet stars, who never frisked about. ______________

8. The mother warned he loved to gobble up comets. ______________

9. The young comet scorned them, but they twinkle every night. ______________

10. Life is no fun unless you venture out. ______________

Personification

Personification is when a writer makes an animal or object behave like a person. In the poem *A Naughty Little Comet*, all the space objects behave like people. They do not behave like normal space objects.

Example: There was once a little comet who lived near the Milky Way!

Comets don't live, and they don't have feelings. These are all things that people do.

List three other examples of personification in the poem.

11. ______________________________

____

12. ______________________________

____

13. ______________________________

____

Score 2 points for each correct answer!

SCORE /26   0-10  12-20  22-26

TARGETING ENGLISH HOMEWORK YEAR 4 © PASCAL PRESS ISBN 978 1 925726 61 9

Phonic & Word Knowledge

UNIT 11

AC9E4LY09, AC9E4LY11

Rhyming words

Write words from the poem that rhyme with these words. Write one more word that rhymes.

1. day ________ ________ ________
2. car ________ ________ ________
3. pup ________ ________ ________
4. here ________ ________ ________
5. tree ________ ________ ________
6. birth ________ ________ ________
7. laze ________ ________ ________
8. mail ________ ________ ________
9. four ________ ________ ________
10. mite ________ ________ ________

Did you notice that not all rhyming words are spelt in the same way?

Homophones

Remember! Homophones are words that sound the same but have a different spelling and meaning.

Write the correct homophone to complete each sentence.

11. The ____________ is the brightest star in the solar system. (Sun, son)
12. The mother took her ____________ to the doctor because he was ill. (Sun, son)
13. The mother said that Sun was an ogre who ____________ on comets. (preys, praise)
14. The little comet earned no ____________ for her bad behaviour. (preys, praise)
15. Stars twinkle in the ____________ sky. (knight, night)
16. A ____________ in shining armour could not defeat the ogre Sun. (knight, night)
17. The naughty little comet disappeared from ____________. (site, sight)
18. You can go stargazing on the ____________ of the old quarry. (site, sight)

Similar words

Choose words from the word bank to complete each sentence.

star	start	stare
stair	steer	stir

19. The little comet liked to make the planets ____________ at her.
20. A gun is fired to ____________ the race.
21. A driver must ____________ the car carefully on the road.
22. It is fun to ____________ chocolate sauce into my ice-cream.
23. She slipped on the bottom ____________ but did not hurt herself.
24. Sirius is the brightest ____________ in the night sky.

Draw lines to match these words to their meanings.

25. reckless	fun, amusement
26. venture	sulk, be sad
27. cautious	careless, irresponsible
28. saucy	careful, wary
29. mirth	happy, joyful (old-fashioned/ dated meaning)
30. wan	cheeky, sassy
31. gay	go, embark
32. mope	pale, weak

The 'sh' sound

Circle the letters that spell the 'sh' sound in these words.

33. wash
34. she
35. cautious
36. show
37. sugar
38. foolish
39. wished
40. vanished

Score 2 points for each correct answer! SCORE /80  0-38   40-74  76-80

TERM 2

Persuasive text – Discussion

Save the Planet, Eat Insects

What would you think if someone gave you a plate of fried crickets for dinner? Most Australians would turn up their noses. However, First Nations Australians have eaten insects for thousands of years. Every day, billions of people eat insects for food. Most of these people live in hot places where there are more insects.

Some scientists suggest we should eat more insects. They say it would help us, and it would help save the planet too.

More than 2,000 species of insects and some spiders are suitable for humans to eat. They include some beetles, butterflies, moths, bees, wasps, ants, grasshoppers, locusts and crickets. They can be eaten whole or ground into flour or used in burgers, pasta and other snacks.

Some people think they must eat meat. But insects are high in protein and nutrients too. And they don't destroy the land the way cattle and sheep do.

If insects were farmed, they would use a lot less land, produce much less greenhouse gas, and provide more nutritious food than livestock does. This would help save our forests. It would reduce the effects of climate change. Food would be more sustainable.

While many people still refuse to try insects, some Australian companies are already using them in types of milk and ice-cream, snacks, and even beer. If people would just try crackers and snacks made from ground-up insects, they would realise how tasty and healthy they are. Maybe then they would try whole insects too. It would be good for us and our planet.

TARGETING ENGLISH HOMEWORK YEAR 4 © PASCAL PRESS ISBN 978 1 925726 61 9

Reading & Comprehension

Shade the bubble next to the correct answer. Write the answer on the line where appropriate.

1. What is the main idea of this article?
   - ◯ that more people should play cricket
   - ◯ that more people should eat insects
   - ◯ that insects are a pest and should be killed

2. What do scientists say?
   - ◯ People are crazy if they eat insects.
   - ◯ Eating insects is good for people and good for the planet.
   - ◯ Insects taste disgusting but are good for you.

3. Where do most of the people who eat insects live?
   - ◯ in Australia
   - ◯ in hot countries
   - ◯ in cities

4. How many species of insects are suitable for people to eat?
   - ◯ 0
   - ◯ 20
   - ◯ 2,000

5. What types of insects are suitable for humans to eat? (Choose any that apply.)
   - ◯ beetles
   - ◯ butterflies
   - ◯ wasps
   - ◯ cockroaches
   - ◯ bees
   - ◯ crickets

6. How can humans eat insects? (Choose any that apply.)
   - ◯ whole
   - ◯ ground into flour
   - ◯ alive
   - ◯ in snacks

7. How does eating more insects help people and the planet? (Choose any that apply.)
   - ◯ They are nutritious.
   - ◯ It helps get rid of annoying insects.
   - ◯ Insects produce less greenhouse gas than cattle and sheep do.
   - ◯ It would reduce the effects of climate change.
   - ◯ Food would be more sustainable.

8. What foods are some Australian companies using insects in? (Choose any that apply.)
   - ◯ milk
   - ◯ ice-cream
   - ◯ snacks
   - ◯ beer
   - ◯ soft drink

9. After reading this article, do you think more people should eat insects?
   - ◯ Yes
   - ◯ No
   - ◯ Unsure

10. Have you ever eaten insects?

    ____

    If 'yes', explain which ones, where and when, and what you thought of them.

    If 'no', would you consider eating them? Explain.

    ____

    ____

    ____

    ____

TERM 2

What I'm reading

Title: ______________________________

It's: ☐ a paper book/magazine/comic
☐ an audiobook
☐ online

It's: ☐ imaginative ☐ informative

Rating ☆ ☆ ☆ ☆ ☆

Score 2 points for each correct answer!

SCORE /20

Grammar & Punctuation

AC9E4LA02, AC9E4LA11, AC9E4LY06

TERM 2

Modal verbs

Modal verbs are helper verbs. They give us more information about the verbs that follow.

Examples:

can could will would

may might should must

Modal verbs can be used to show:

- how likely something is to happen (Most Australians **would** turn up their noses.)
- someone's ability to do something (People **can** eat insects for food.)
- if something must be done (Some people think they **must** eat meat.)
- if permission is given to do something (Some people **may** eat insects instead of meat.)
- if something is planned to be done (In the future, insects **will** become a common source of food.)

Write modal verbs to complete these sentences

1. People _______________ like insects for food if they try them.
2. If insects were farmed, they _______________ use a lot less land than livestock.
3. In the future, more and more people _______________ eat insects for food.
4. You _______________ already try insects in some snacks, including ice-cream.
5. Insects _______________ be eaten whole or ground into flour.
6. People might like insects if they _______________ just try them.
7. People _______________ eat more insects!
8. We _______________ do more to make food more sustainable.
9. I think I _______________ try some insect snacks.
10. I _______________ rather try insects in snacks first.

Thinking verbs

Thinking verbs tell us about the thinking that is being done.

Examples:

think believe wonder suggest

know forget understand forgive

imagine realise notice guess

Circle the thinking verbs in these sentences.

11. Most Australians don't think of insects as food.
12. Some scientists suggest we should eat more insects.
13. I wonder if more people will eat insects in the future.
14. I know that a lot of people all over the world already eat insects as food.
15. People understand that there are many benefits of eating insects as food.
16. Not everyone believes that it is necessary to eat meat.
17. I guess it might be fun to try insects in snack foods first.
18. I didn't notice that these crackers were made with insect flour.
19. I can't imagine a world without insects.
20. People must realise that eating insects is healthy.

Topic words

Draw lines to match these words to their meanings.

21. scientist	right or appropriate
22. species	an essential building block for life
23. suitable	gases that trap heat in the atmosphere
24. protein	a person who studies science
25. nutrients	farm animals
26. greenhouse gas	a group of living things that share characteristics
27. livestock	substances that provide nourishment

Score 2 points for each correct answer!

SCORE /54

0-24

26-48

50-54

TARGETING ENGLISH HOMEWORK YEAR 4 © PASCAL PRESS ISBN 978 1 925726 61 9

Phonic & Word Knowledge

UNIT 12

AC9E4LY09, AC9E4LY10, AC9E4LY11

Word origins

Some of the words we use in English today come from other languages.

Examples: **Science** comes from the **Latin** word *scientia*, which means 'knowledge'.

Protein comes from the **Greek** word *proteios*, which means 'primary' or 'in the lead', as proteins are important for life.

Where words originated often influences their spelling and/or their pronunciation.

Words that begin with 'sc'

The letters 'sc' at the beginning of a word usually spell a blend 's+k' in which both letters are pronounced.

Example: **sc**at

Sometimes the letters 'sch' also spell the blend.

Example: **sch**ool

In some words, the letters 'sc' spell a digraph with the 's' sound. *Example:* **sc**ience

A digraph 's' sound usually precedes an 'e' or an 'i'.

Say these words that begin with the letters 'sc'. Write SK if you hear the blend. Write S if you hear the digraph.

1. _____ science
2. _____ scoop
3. _____ scale
4. _____ scene
5. _____ scar
6. _____ scout
7. _____ scientist
8. _____ scooter
9. _____ scent
10. _____ scissors

Homophones – Scent, sent or cent

Choose the correct word to complete each sentence.

11. When ladybirds are afraid, they release a strange _______________.
12. My father showed me a collection of one _______________ coins from his childhood.
13. I _______________ an e-card to my grandmother for her birthday.

Compound words

Draw lines to match the beginning and end words to form compound words.

14. butter	be
15. green	stock
16. how	one
17. may	fly
18. grass	hopper
19. live	house
20. some	ever

The suffix 'ion'

In many two-syllable words that end with the suffix 'ion', the final syllable contains the schwa 'uh' sound. The syllable usually sounds like y + uh + n, like in billion.

Sometimes when the word ends with 'tion', the syllable sounds like sh + uh + n, like in station.

Read these words. Write 'yuhn' or 'shun' depending on the sound you hear.

21. _____ million
22. _____ union
23. _____ opinion
24. _____ station
25. _____ potion
26. _____ nation
27. _____ pavilion
28. _____ addition
29. _____ vacation
30. _____ trillion

Score 2 points for each correct answer! SCORE /60  0-28  30-54  56-60 

TERM 2

AC9E4LA03, AC9E4LA10, AC9E4LY03, AC9E4LY04, AC9E4LY05

Informative text – Report

TERM 2

The Cook Islands

The Cook Islands are in the South Pacific Ocean. They are north-east of New Zealand. They lie between French Polynesia and Fiji.

The Cook Islands are made up of 15 small islands. They are divided into two groups – the Lower Cook Islands and the Northern Cook Islands.

The capital city is Avarua. It is located on the main island of Rarotonga.

Most of the people live on the southern islands.

There are three main languages spoken in the Cook Islands – Maori, English and Pukapukan.

The Cook Islands were first settled by Polynesian people. They migrated by boat from other Pacific islands around 800 AD.

The British took control of the Cook Islands in 1888 but passed control to New Zealand in 1901. The Cook Islands became an independent nation in 1965.

The islands were named after Captain James Cook. He was the first European to explore the islands in the 1770s.

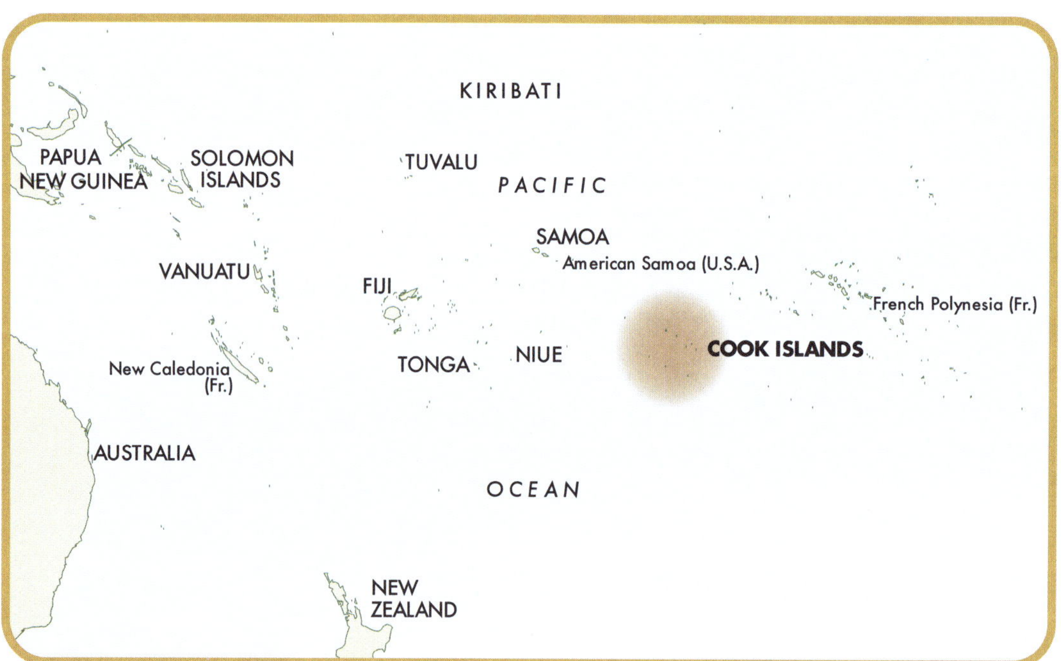

Source: Text and image from *Rhythm and Dance, Polynesian Culture*, by Rita Faelli, Blake Education.

TARGETING ENGLISH HOMEWORK YEAR 4 © PASCAL PRESS ISBN 978 1 925726 61 9

Reading & Comprehension

Shade the bubble next to the correct answer.

1. Where are the Cook Islands located?
   - ◯ in the Pacific Ocean
   - ◯ in the Atlantic Ocean
   - ◯ in New Zealand

2. In which part of the world are the Cook Islands?
   - ◯ the Northern Hemisphere
   - ◯ the Southern Hemisphere
   - ◯ Antarctica

3. How many islands are in the Cook Islands?
   - ◯ 2
   - ◯ 15
   - ◯ 30

4. Which of these is **not** a group of islands in the Cook Islands?
   - ◯ the Lower Cook Islands
   - ◯ the Northern Cook Islands
   - ◯ Rarotonga

5. What is the **capital** of the Cook Islands?
   - ◯ Fiji
   - ◯ Avarua
   - ◯ Rarotonga

6. Which are the three main languages spoken in the Cook Islands?
   - ◯ Maori, English, Pukapukan
   - ◯ French, English, Maori
   - ◯ Maori, French, Pukapukan

7. Where did the **first settlers** of the Cook Islands come from?
   - ◯ Britian
   - ◯ Polynesia
   - ◯ New Zealand

8. How did the Polynesian settlers get to the Cook Islands?
   - ◯ by foot
   - ◯ by boat
   - ◯ by plane

9. When did the Cook Islands become an independent nation?
   - ◯ 800 AD
   - ◯ 1888
   - ◯ 1965

10. Why are the islands called the Cook Islands?
    - ◯ because the people are good cooks
    - ◯ after Captain James Cook
    - ◯ because it's very hot on the islands

TERM 2

Score 2 points for each correct answer! SCORE /20   

Grammar & Punctuation

AC9E4LA04, AC9E4LA12, AC9E4LY06

Noun groups – Determiners

Remember! A noun group is a group of words built around a noun. The noun is the main word and the words in the noun group give more information about the noun.

A determiner is part of a noun group. Its job is to point out (determine) the noun.

Examples: **his** boat **this** island **most** people

Examples of determiners: the, a, an, this, that, these, those, some, most, every, each, any, my, your, her, his, its, our, their, whose, what, which, one, two, three.

TERM 2

Circle the nouns and underline the determiners in the noun groups in these sentences.

1. Most people live on the southern islands.
2. The three main languages are Maori, English and Pukapukan.
3. The capital city is Avarua.
4. The Cook Islands became an independent nation in 1965.
5. The Cook Islands is a group of 15 small islands.

Classifiers

A classifier is placed before the main noun to say what type it is.

Examples: the **capital** city the **main** island

Add classifiers to complete these sentences from the text. Circle the nouns they describe.

6. The ______________ settlers were Polynesian people.
7. The Cook Islands are made up of fifteen ______________ islands.
8. Three ______________ languages are spoken on the islands.
9. The Cook Islands became an ______________ nation in 1965.
10. The Polynesian people migrated by boat from other ______________ islands.

Proper nouns

Remember! Proper nouns are the names of particular people, places, objects and events. Proper nouns begin with a capital letter.

The capital letters are missing from the proper nouns in these sentences. Rewrite the sentences correctly, including a capital letter to begin the sentence and a full stop at the end.

11. the cook islands is a group of 15 islands in the south pacific ocean

____

____

____

12. the capital city avarua is on the main island of rarotonga

____

____

____

13. the three main languages are maori, english and pukapukan

____

____

____

14. the islands were named after captain james cook

____

____

____

15. new zealand was in charge of the cook islands from 1888 until 1965

____

____

____

Score 2 points for each correct answer! SCORE  /30  0-12  14-24  26-30

TARGETING ENGLISH HOMEWORK YEAR 4 © PASCAL PRESS ISBN 978 1 925726 61 9

Phonic & Word Knowledge

AC9E4LY09, AC9E4LY10

Syllables

Breaking words into syllables can be helpful when you are reading words from other languages. However, the pronunciation may be different in the original language.

Reminder:

Double consonants: Break between the consonants.

Two or more consonants: Break between the consonants, but do not split a digraph or blend.

Vowels: Break before the consonant if the vowel sound is long. Break after the consonant if the vowel sound is short.

Break these words into syllables using the rules above. For each word, write the number of syllables, then show the syllables separated by a + sign.

1. _____ Zealand _____
2. _____ Fiji _____
3. _____ lower _____
4. _____ capital _____
5. _____ English _____
6. _____ control _____
7. _____ Raratonga _____
8. _____ Pukapukan _____
9. _____ Pacific _____
10. _____ independent _____

Verb tense – Adding 'ed' and 'ing'

Add endings to these base verbs to show past tense and present tense. Don't be tricked. Some verbs are irregular in the past tense.

	Base verb	Did (past tense)	Doing now (present tense)
11	settle		
12	migrate		
13	live		
14	divide		
15	make		
16	speak		
17	control		
18	pass		
19	explore		
20	become		

Past tense of regular verbs

Say the words in the word bank. Underline the 'ed' ending. Sort the words into the table according to the sound represented by 'ed'.

migrated	named	divided
passed	located	settled
controlled	looked	faced

	't'
21	
22	
23	
	'd'
24	
25	
26	
	'id'
27	
28	
29	

Score 2 points for each correct answer! SCORE /58 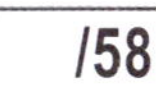 0-26  28-52  54-58 

TERM 2

Informative text – Explanation

Heatwaves

What is a heatwave?

A heatwave is very hot weather that lasts for five or more days.

Heatwaves usually occur in summer when a high pressure system makes the air and ground extremely hot. If there is no wind to shift the pressure system away, it can last for days.

Heatwave effects

Heatwaves can have a disastrous effect on all living things, including humans. The effects are worse if the humidity is high and people can't cool down. During heatwaves, people use their air conditioners more. The surge in electricity needed can cause power outages.

If people get too hot and stop sweating, they may suffer heatstroke. It can be fatal. The very young, very old and sick people are more at risk. Heatwaves can also cause wildfires and bushfires that destroy large areas of land and property.

Worst heatwaves

In August 2003, a severe heatwave swept across Europe. Temperatures in some regions were over 40° for two weeks. More than 52,000 people died. It was the hottest weather Europe had experienced for at least 500 years.

In March 2008, Adelaide set the record for the longest-lasting heatwave of an Australian capital city. It had 15 consecutive days over 35°. It was described as a "once in three thousand years" event.

Climate scientists consider 2023 to be the hottest year. As temperatures continue to rise across the world, we can expect there to be more and more severe heatwaves in the future.

Source: Text adapted from *Weather*, a Go Facts Climate book, Blake Education.

TARGETING ENGLISH HOMEWORK YEAR 4 © PASCAL PRESS ISBN 978 1 925726 61 9

Reading & Comprehension

Shade the bubble next to the correct answer. Write the answer on the line where appropriate.

1. When do heat waves usually occur?
   - ◯ during summer
   - ◯ during spring
   - ◯ during autumn

2. A heatwave is declared when the weather is:
   - ◯ very hot.
   - ◯ very hot for five or more days.
   - ◯ very hot for ten days.

3. Which of these is **not** a condition of a heatwave?
   - ◯ high pressure system
   - ◯ very hot air and ground
   - ◯ strong winds

4. What makes the effects of heatwaves worse?
   - ◯ high humidity
   - ◯ air conditioning
   - ◯ sweat

5. What happens when someone has **heatstroke**? (Choose any that apply.)
   - ◯ They get too hot.
   - ◯ They stop sweating.
   - ◯ They may die.

6. When did **Europe** suffer a severe heatwave?
   - ◯ 500 years ago
   - ◯ 52 years ago
   - ◯ in 2003

7. When was Australia's worst heatwave?
   - ◯ 2003
   - ◯ 2008
   - ◯ 2023

8. How long was Australia's worst heatwave?
   - ◯ 5 days
   - ◯ 15 days
   - ◯ 35 days

9. What was the hottest year on record up until 2023?
   - ◯ 2003
   - ◯ 2008
   - ◯ 2023

10. Have you ever experienced extremely hot weather? ______________________

    How did or would you feel?

    ____

    ____

    What did you do, or would you do, to cool down?

    ____

    ____

    ____

    ____

    ____

    ____

    ____

    ____

TERM 2

What I'm reading

Title: ______________________

It's: ☐ a paper book/magazine/comic
☐ an audiobook
☐ online

It's: ☐ imaginative ☐ informative

Rating ☆ ☆ ☆ ☆ ☆

Score 2 points for each correct answer!

SCORE /20

Grammar & Punctuation

AC9E4LA06, AC9E4LA12, AC9E4LY06

Complex sentences

Remember! A clause is a group of words with one subject and one verb.

A simple sentence consists of one clause. Because it makes sense on its own, it is an independent clause.

Example: A heatwave is very hot weather.

A compound sentence is made up of two simple sentences. They are both independent clauses as each clause would make sense on its own. They are joined by a conjunction.

Example: A heatwave is very hot weather, **and** it usually occurs in summer.

A complex sentence is also made up of two or more clauses. In a complex sentence, there is one clause that tells the main idea. It is called the main clause or the principal clause. It makes sense on its own.

A subordinate or dependent clause gives more information about the main idea in the principal clause. Subordinate or dependent clauses do not make sense on their own. They may be linked to the principal clause by a conjunction or a relative pronoun.

Example: A heatwave is very hot weather **that** lasts for five or more days.

TERM 2

Read these complex sentences. Circle the verbs. Underline the principal clause. Highlight the conjunction or relative pronouns used to link the clauses.

1. Heatwaves usually occur in summer when the air and ground is extremely hot.
2. It can last for days if there is no wind.
3. People may suffer heatstroke when they get too hot.
4. Heatwaves can cause bushfires that destroy large areas of land and property.
5. We can expect more severe heatwaves as temperatures continue to rise across the world.

Read these sentences. Circle the verbs. Write S for a simple sentence, C for a compound sentence and X for a complex sentence.

6. _____ Heatwaves can have a disastrous effect on all living things, including humans.
7. _____ The effects are worse if the humidity is high.
8. _____ The very young, very old and sick people are more at risk.
9. _____ During heatwaves, people use their air conditioners more and that can cause power outages.
10. _____ If there is no wind to shift the pressure system away, it can last for days.

Add a subordinate clause to each of these independent clauses to form a complex sentence. Make sure your clause has a verb.

11. More than 52 000 people died **when** ______________________
12. Climate scientists say there will be more and more heatwaves **because** ______________________
13. In 2008 Adelaide had Australia's longest heatwave **that** ______________________
14. Heatstroke can be fatal **if** ______________________
15. We can stay cool inside with an air conditioner **although** ______________________

Proper nouns

There are 4 proper nouns in the text. Can you find them all? Write them here.

16. ______________________

Score 2 points for each correct answer!

SCORE /32  0-14  16-26  28-32

TARGETING ENGLISH HOMEWORK YEAR 4 © PASCAL PRESS ISBN 978 1 925726 61 9

Phonic & Word Knowledge

AC9E4LY09

Compound words

Write fire in front or at the end of these words to make a compound word. Draw lines to match the words to their illustration.

1. fighter ______________
2. bush ______________
3. cracker ______________
4. camp ______________
5. fly ______________

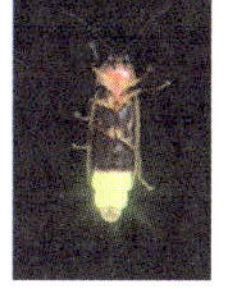

The sounds s, sh and z

The letter 's' usually represents the 's' sound we hear at the beginning of snake.

We usually use the letters 'sh' to spell the sound we hear at the beginning of ship.

And the letter 'z' is usually used to represent the 'z' sound we hear at the beginning of zoo.

But that is not always the case.

Say these words. Look at the letters in bold type. Write S if you hear the 's' sound, SH if you hear the 'sh' sound, and Z if you hear the 'z' sound.

6. _____ **sh**ift
7. _____ u**s**e
8. _____ day**s**
9. _____ **s**ick
10. _____ pre**ss**ure
11. _____ week**s**
12. _____ **s**urge
13. _____ cau**s**e
14. _____ condi**ti**oner

Words that end with 'le'

When the letters 'le' occur at the end of a word, they make the 'l' sound.

Example: peop**le**

Say the words in the word bank. Choose a word to complete each sentence.

people	settle	bubble	turtle
whistle	table	puddle	
cable	nibble	middle	

15. It is fun to have a ______________ bath when it is hot.
16. Most ______________ stay indoors when there is a heatwave.
17. The mother ______________ lays her eggs in the sand.
18. A duck splashed in a ______________ on the road after the rains came.
19. My grandfather likes to ______________ while he works.
20. One of my jobs at home is to set the ______________ for dinner.

Words that end with 'tion'

When the letters 'tion' occur at the end of a word, they often sound like 'shun' with a schwa sound.

Example: condi**tion**

Draw lines to match the words with their meanings.

21. decoration	a holiday
22. potion	feelings
23. vacation	an ornament or trimming to beautify
24. education	a liquid mixture
25. emotion	learning

Score 2 points for each correct answer! SCORE /50

TERM 2

AC9E4LA03, AC9E4LY03, AC9E4LY04, AC9E4LY05

Imaginative text – Science Fiction

The Silver Ball of Hope (Part 2)

(You can read other chapters of this story in Units 7, 23 & 31)

Tor and Cassi set out for the Gravalon Crater to find the silver ball of hope.

"YOU, little brother, are not coming!" says Tor firmly. "You are going to stay here and stay out of trouble!"

"It's not fair," Cha grumbles as he watches them through the viewing port. They move carefully among the rocks and craters and soon disappear into the Gravalon Crater. He feels very alone as he sits on the top step of the spaceship.

In the distance, Cha sees a reddish glow. Curious, he decides to investigate. He jumps down into the Mylos dust.

Suddenly, a gust of wind picks him up and carries him into a forest. Vines and creepers snake through the trees. Soft grasses and ferns cover the forest floor. Cha sees some golden flowers high up in a tree.

"I know," thinks Cha. "I'll give Cass some flowers. That will get me back on side."

He grabs a vine and starts to climb when he hears something thumping through the bushes. He scurries down, and still clutching the vine, escapes out of the forest. But when he looks around, all he can see is empty land dotted with rocks and craters. The spaceship is nowhere in sight.

"Uh-oh! Now I really AM in trouble!" he mutters.

Source: Image from and text adapted from *The Silver Ball of Hope*, the second book in the Star Quest series by Del Merrick, Blake Education.

TARGETING ENGLISH HOMEWORK YEAR 4 © PASCAL PRESS ISBN 978 1 925726 61 9

Reading & Comprehension

Use these clues to complete the crossword.

Across

1. Cha was told to stay in the __________.
5. A __________ of wind picked Cha up.
7. Tor told Cha to stay out of __________.
9. Cha grabbed a __________.
12. The wind took Cha into a __________.
14. Cha felt very __________ left in the spaceship.
15. Cha saw a __________ glow.

Down

2. Cha watched through the viewing __________.
3. Cha went to __________ a reddish glow.
4. Cha was __________ about the reddish glow.
6. Many tall __________ grew in the forest.
8. Cha is Tor's __________.
10. Cha thought it was __________ to be left behind.
11. Tor and Cassi went into the Gravalon __________.
13. Cha __________ some golden flowers.

TERM 2

1	2						3			4		
									5			6
	7				8				9			
10												
		11										
12												
											13	
							14					
						15						

What I'm reading

Title: ______________________

It's: ☐ a paper book/magazine/comic
☐ an audiobook
☐ online

It's: ☐ imaginative ☐ informative

Rating ☆ ☆ ☆ ☆ ☆

Score 2 points for each correct answer!

SCORE /30 0-12 14-24 26-30

Grammar & Punctuation

AC9E4LA06, AC9E4LA07

Direct speech – Speech marks, commas, capital letters

Remember! Writers use speech marks, also called quotation marks ("…") at the beginning and end of what characters say. The first spoken word always has a capital letter. A comma marks off the spoken words from the rest of the sentence unless a question mark (?) or exclamation mark (!) is used.

Saying verbs show which people are talking and how they say things.

Add the missing capital letters, speech marks and other punctuation where necessary. Circle the saying verbs.

1. you are not coming says Tor firmly
2. it's not fair Cha grumbles
3. I wonder what that is says Cha to himself
4. I know thinks Cha I'll give Cass some flowers
5. Now I really am in trouble Cha mutters

Saying verbs

said	shouted	pleaded	suggested
cried	yelled	mumbled	spluttered
muttered	joked	laughed	whispered
answered	argued	commanded	
insisted	sighed	screamed	asked

Choose saying verbs from the box to complete these sentences.

6. "Don't leave me behind," ______________ Cha.
7. "I think there's something out there," ______________ Cassi.
8. "Don't go anywhere!" ______________ Tor.
9. "Why didn't you do as you were told?" ______________ Tor.
10. "I'm really sorry," ______________ Cha. "I didn't mean to."

Compound sentences

Remember! A compound sentence is made up of two independent clauses joined by a joining word (also called a conjunction).

We can use the acronym FANBOYS to help us remember the conjunctions: for, and, nor, but, or, yet, so.

Sometimes, if the subject is repeated, it is omitted in the second clause. It is understood.

Example: **You** are going to stay here and (you) stay out of trouble.

Underline the two independent clauses in these sentences. Circle the conjunction. Use a caret ^ to write in the subject if it has been omitted.

11. They move carefully among the rocks and craters and soon disappear into the Gravalon Crater.
12. A gust of wind picks him up and carries him into a forest.
13. He grabs a vine and starts to climb.

14. He scurries down and escapes out of the forest.
15. The spaceship has disappeared and is nowhere in sight.

Score 2 points for each correct answer!

SCORE /30  0-12  14-24  26-30

TERM 2

TARGETING ENGLISH HOMEWORK YEAR 4 © PASCAL PRESS ISBN 978 1 925726 61 9

Phonic & Word Knowledge

AC9E4LY09, AC9E4LY10, AC9E4LY11

Plurals

To make a word plural (more than one), you usually just add **-s**. For words that end in ch, sh, s, ss, x, z or zz, you add **-es** to make them plural.

Examples: ball**s**, spaceship**s**, tree**s**, dish**es**, box**es**

Some words do not follow the rules.

Examples: ox – oxen   quiz – quizzes

Some words do not change for the plural.

Examples: fish, sheep

Write the plural of these words.

1. step ______________________
2. crater ______________________
3. bush ______________________
4. noise ______________________
5. rock ______________________
6. grass ______________________
7. forest ______________________
8. fern ______________________
9. buzz ______________________
10. gust ______________________

The suffix 'ish'

The suffix 'ish' is added to a word to make a new word. It has different meanings.

Examples:

Nationality: British, Spanish

Similar to or **like**: childish, greenish

Roughly or **about**: smallish, 2-ish (about 2 o'clock)

The rules for adding 'ish' to words are similar to those for adding other suffixes such as 'ed' and 'ing'. However, sometimes the base word may change, especially with nationalities.

Add the suffix 'ish' to each of these words to make a new word.

11. red ______________________
12. book ______________________
13. dry ______________________
14. boy ______________________
15. big ______________________
16. strong ______________________

Choose 'ish' words from 11 – 16 to complete these sentences.

17. My sister is very sporty but my brother is more ______________________.
18. Cha saw a ______________________ glow in the distance.
19. A ______________________ wind picked Cha up and carried him into the forest.
20. Something ______________________ was thumping through the forest.

Short vowel sound 'u' in words that end in 'le'

In most words with the short vowel sound 'u' that end in 'le', the sound is written with the letter 'u'.

Examples: b**u**bble, p**u**zzle

Other words break this rule and represent the sound with the vowel digraph 'ou'.

Examples: tr**ou**ble, d**ou**ble, c**ou**ple

Write the letter or letters to complete these words. Draw lines to match words to their pictures.

21. b___bble
22. d___ble
23. b___ckle
24. cr___mble
25. c___ple

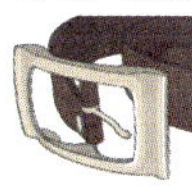

Score 2 points for each correct answer! SCORE /50

TERM 2

AC9E4LA02, AC9E4LE03

TV show review: *Horrible Histories*

Horrible Histories

You can watch ***Horrible Histories*** *on ABC iView.*

Reviewed by Ethan, 10, New South Wales

Horrible Histories is my favourite show. I've read lots of the books, so now I'm watching the TV shows. They are so funny.

I love the way they tell things that happened in the past. It is hard to believe that some of these things really happened.

My friends like to watch *Horrible Histories* too. Sometimes we watch episodes over and over. We can watch them on YouTube too. We have fun learning the songs off by heart, like the Charles II rap song. Lately, we've been trying to remember the Monarch's song. I can name nearly all the English kings and queens in order. I couldn't do that without *Horrible Histories*.

You can learn so much from watching the show. I liked the one when Rattus was looking for a new job. He told us about so many weird jobs. I couldn't imagine anyone wanting to do them, like carrying a bucket around for people to use as a toilet. Yuck! But it was true.

If you like history, or even if you don't, I think you'll really like *Horrible Histories*. You'll laugh a lot, but you'll learn a lot too.

I recommend it for children over 8 because some parts are a bit gory.

I give it 5 stars.

TARGETING ENGLISH HOMEWORK YEAR 4 © PASCAL PRESS ISBN 978 1 925726 61 9

Review

Shade the bubble next to the correct answer. Write the answer on the line where appropriate.

1. Have you watched any episodes of *Horrible Histories*?
   - ◯ Yes
   - ◯ No
   - ◯ Unsure

2. After reading this review, do you think you will watch some episodes of *Horrible Histories*?
   - ◯ Yes
   - ◯ No
   - ◯ Unsure

3. Which words or phrases in the review help you decide?

   ____

   ____

   ____

   ____

4. List some TV shows that you like to watch. Circle your favourite.

   ____

   ____

   ____

   ____

   ____

Now you can write a review of your favourite TV show so that others can decide whether to watch it or not.

1. About the TV show

   Title: ______________________________

   Where can you watch it? ______________________________

   ____

2. Circle the word that best describes the category of TV show.

   comedy science fiction superhero
   family adventure mystery scary
   detective education action
   nature history

   If the type of TV show is not listed, write it here: ______________________________

3. How is the TV show presented? (Choose any that apply.)
   - ◯ animated
   - ◯ puppets
   - ◯ real people or animals
   - ◯ people acting
   - ◯ other ______________________________

4. Which of these is true about the show?
   - ◯ Each episode has a separate story or adventure.
   - ◯ The episodes follow each other to tell one continuous story.
   - ◯ Each episode has a series of mini stories or adventures.
   - ◯ other ______________________________

5. How long have you been watching the show? ______________________________

6. How often do you watch the show?

   ____

7. Who do you watch the show with?

   ____

8. Where do you watch the show?

   ____

The characters

9. What do you know about the main character; for example, their name, where they live, what they like doing, what they look like? Include anything you find interesting about the character.

   ____

   ____

   ____

   ____

   ____

   ____

   ____

   ____

   ____

   ____

TERM 2

Review

⑩ What do you know about one of the supporting characters; for example, their name, where they live, what they like doing, what they look like? Include anything you find interesting about the character.

⑪ Who is your favourite character?

Why?

⑫ What sorts of things do the characters do in every episode?

The setting

⑬ When does the TV show take place?

- ◯ in the past, a long time ago
- ◯ in the past, not long ago
- ◯ in the present
- ◯ in the future
- ◯ not sure

⑭ Where does the TV show take place? Is it a real location or a fictional place?

⑮ List things that can be seen, heard or smelled in the location.

Seen

Heard

Smelled

TARGETING ENGLISH HOMEWORK YEAR 4 © PASCAL PRESS ISBN 978 1 925726 61 9

Review

The plot

⑯ Describe the types of things that happen in each episode or choose one episode and tell about it. Include what happens at the beginning, what problems occur, and how the episode concludes or usually concludes.

⑰ What do you like best about this TV show?

Draw a picture of a favourite scene.

⑱ Is this show like any other shows you have watched? If so, in what way?

⑲ Who else might like to watch it? Who do you recommend it for?

⑳ How many stars do you give it?

☆☆☆☆☆

Reading & Comprehension

Boomerangs

First Nations Australians have made boomerangs for thousands of years.

Boomerangs are made from the curved root of a mulga, mangrove or wattle tree. The edge of a boomerang is shaped like the wing of an aeroplane. When it is thrown properly, a boomerang returns to the thrower. Other types of throwing sticks are designed to fly in a straight line and kill or stun the animals they strike.

Boomerangs are also used as clapping sticks and digging tools.

When the first British people arrived in Australia, they saw and described boomerangs. They became popular souvenirs in the nineteenth century. They were a symbol of returning home. Many houses, hotels and ships were named "Boomerang". Some airlines used boomerangs to advertise flights that would take passengers "there and back".

The only fighter plane that was designed and built in Australia was named the "Boomerang". During World War I, some volunteers who fought for Australia were called "boomerang marchers". They received a boomerang-shaped medal with the words "Come back" on it.

Source: Image from and text adapted from *Symbols of Australia* by Mark Stafford, Go Facts Australia, Blake Education.

TERM 2

Shade the bubble next to the correct answer.

1. **Who makes boomerangs?**
   - ◯ First Nations Australians
   - ◯ British people
   - ◯ anyone in Australia

2. **How long have they been making boomerangs?**
   - ◯ since the first British people arrived
   - ◯ for thousands of years
   - ◯ since World War I

3. **Which of these trees is not used to make boomerangs?**
   - ◯ mulga
   - ◯ mangrove
   - ◯ eucalyptus

4. **What is the edge of a boomerang shaped like?**
   - ◯ a knife
   - ◯ a wing
   - ◯ an arrow

5. **What does a boomerang do when it is used properly?**
   - ◯ return to the thrower
   - ◯ fly in a straight line
   - ◯ kill an animal

6. **Which of these are not uses of boomerangs?**
   - ◯ sun protection
   - ◯ clapping sticks
   - ◯ digging sticks

7. **When did boomerangs become popular as souvenirs?**
   - ◯ thousands of years ago
   - ◯ in the nineteenth century
   - ◯ after World War I

8. **What are boomerangs a symbol of?**
   - ◯ being Australian
   - ◯ being homesick
   - ◯ returning home

9. **What was the name of the only fighter plane designed and built in Australia?**
   - ◯ Boomerang
   - ◯ Australia I
   - ◯ Boomerang Flyer

10. **What did the volunteers known as boomerang marchers receive?**
    - ◯ a boomerang
    - ◯ a medal
    - ◯ a model aeroplane

Score 2 points for each correct answer! SCORE /20 0-8 10-14 16-20

TARGETING ENGLISH HOMEWORK YEAR 4 © PASCAL PRESS ISBN 978 1 925726 61 9

Grammar & Punctuation

Sentence types

Read these sentences. Circle the verbs. Write S for a simple sentence, C for a compound sentence and X for a complex sentence.

1. _____ First Nations Australians have made boomerangs for thousands of years.
2. _____ A boomerang returns to the thrower when it is thrown properly.
3. _____ Other throwing sticks fly in a straight line and may kill the animals they strike.
4. _____ Boomerangs are also used as clapping sticks and digging tools.
5. _____ When the first British people arrived in Australia, they saw and described boomerangs.
6. _____ They became popular souvenirs in the nineteenth century.
7. _____ Boomerangs are made from the curved root of a mulga, mangrove or wattle tree.
8. _____ Some airlines used boomerangs to advertise flights that would take passengers “there and back”.
9. _____ The only fighter plane that was designed and built in Australia was named the "Boomerang".
10. _____ The volunteers were called “boomerang marchers” and they received a boomerang-shaped medal.

Verbs – Singular and plural

Choose the correct verb to complete each sentence.

11. Boomerangs _______________ been made for thousands of years. (has/have)
12. A boomerang _______________ back if it is thrown properly. (comes, come)
13. The edge of a boomerang _______________ shaped like a wing. (is, are)
14. Boomerangs _______________ popular souvenirs. (is, are)
15. First Nations Australians _______________ boomerangs. (makes, make)

Adverbial phrases

Underline the adverbial phrase in each sentence. Circle the preposition. Write what the adverbial phrase tells about the verb: H (how), T (time/when), P (place/where), W (why).

16. _____ First Nations Australians have made boomerangs for thousands of years.
17. _____ Boomerangs are made from the curved root of a tree.
18. _____ Other types of throwing sticks are designed to fly in a straight line.
19. _____ After their arrival in Australia, British people wanted boomerangs as souvenirs.
20. _____ They became popular souvenirs in the nineteenth century.

Pronouns

Circle the pronouns in these sentences. Write the noun they replace.

21. They have made boomerangs for thousands of years. _______________
22. They are made from the curved roots of trees. _______________
23. It will come back if thrown properly. _______________
24. You can buy boomerangs in souvenirs shops. _______________
25. Many people who were homesick bought souvenir boomerangs. _______________

Modal verbs

Write a modal verb to complete these sentences.

26. You ____________ buy boomerangs in souvenir stores.
27. You ____________ be careful when you are throwing boomerangs.
28. I ____________ name my bicycle “The Boomerang”.
29. We ____________ learn how to throw boomerangs next term.
30. If a boomerang is thrown properly, it ____________ come back to the thrower.

Verb types

Read these verbs. Write D for doing, S for saying, T for thinking.

31. _____ jump
32. _____ imagine
33. _____ yell
34. _____ remember
35. _____ exclaim
36. _____ mutter
37. _____ fly
38. _____ wonder
39. _____ clap

Grammar & Punctuation

Noun groups

Underline the **noun groups** in these sentences. Highlight the **noun**. Draw a box around the **determiner** and circle the **classifier**.

40. Boomerangs are made from a curved root.
41. A souvenir boomerang can be bought in a shop.
42. Other throwing sticks fly in a straight line.
43. Boomerangs are used as clapping sticks sometimes.
44. The first British people arrived in Australia in 1778.
45. Boomerangs are made by First Nations Australians.

Punctuation

The capital letters are missing from the **proper nouns** in these sentences. Rewrite the sentences correctly, including a **capital letter** to begin the sentence and a **full stop** at the end.

46. boomerangs have been made by first nations australians for thousands of years

____

____

47. the first british people were fascinated by boomerangs

____

____

48. the boomerang was designed and made in australia in world war I

____

____

Punctuation with direct speech

Add the missing **capital letters, speech marks** and other punctuation where necessary. Circle the **saying verbs.**

49. i am learning to throw a boomerang so it will come back said jai
50. watch out called Tan as the boomerang swung round

Score 2 points for each correct answer!

Phonic & Word Knowledge

Long vowel sounds

Say the words in the word bank. Sort them into the table according to the long vowel sounds you can hear.

throw	boomerang	use	root
plane	saw	straight	thousands
type	souvenirs	popular	now
people	flights	fought	houses
for	tree	receive	they
hotels	design	new	only

1 long 'a' as in cake			
2 long 'e' as in bee			
3 long 'i' as in bike			
4 long 'o' as in goat			
5 long 'u' as in mule			
6 long 'oo' as in moon			
7 'or' as in four			
8 'ow' as in cow			

TERM 2

TARGETING ENGLISH HOMEWORK YEAR 4 © PASCAL PRESS ISBN 978 1 925726 61 9

Phonic & Word Knowledge

Schwa sound

Break these words into **syllables**. Circle the unstressed syllable. Write the letter or letters that represent the **schwa sound**.

9. mulga = ________ + ________ (_____)
10. symbol = ________ + ________ (_____)
11. houses = ________ + ________ (_____)
12. medal = ________ + ________ (_____)

Past tense of regular verbs

Read these words. Write **t**, **d**, or **id** for the sound made by the ending 'ed'.

13. curved _____
14. intended _____
15. designed _____
16. shaped _____
17. started _____
18. arrived _____
19. liked _____
20. landed _____
21. watched _____

Homophones

Write the correct **homophone** to complete each sentence.

22. Some volunteers who ______________ in the war were called 'boomerang marchers'. (fort, fought)
23. The "boomerang marchers" fought ______________ Australia. (for, four)
24. People ______________ buy boomerangs as souvenirs. (wood, would)
25. The "boomerang marchers" wore ______________ medals proudly. (their, there)
26. The only fighter plane ______________ in Australia was called the "Boomerang". (made, maid)

Verb tense – Adding 'ed' and 'ing'

Add endings to these base verbs to show **past tense** and **present tense**. Don't be tricked. Some verbs are irregular in the past tense.

	Base verb	Did (past tense)	Doing now (present tense)
27	make		
28	shape		
29	throw		
30	return		
31	fly		
32	use		
33	fight		

S, sh and z

Say these words. Look at the letters in bold type. Write **S** if you hear the 's' sound, **SH** if you hear the 'sh' sound, and **Z** if you hear the 'z' sound.

34. _____ thousands
35. _____ **s**ticks
36. _____ adverti**s**e
37. _____ **sh**ape
38. _____ na**t**ion
39. _____ de**s**ign
40. _____ type**s**
41. _____ **s**traight
42. _____ **sh**ip

Plurals

Write the **plural** of these words.

43. root ______________________
44. tree ______________________
45. grass ______________________
46. bush ______________________
47. boomerang ______________________
48. type ______________________
49. stick ______________________
50. plane ______________________
51. medal ______________________
52. thousand ______________________

Score 2 points for each correct answer!

TARGETING ENGLISH HOMEWORK YEAR 4 © PASCAL PRESS ISBN 978 1 925726 61 9

Reading & Comprehension

AC9E4LA03, AC9E4LY03, AC9E4LY04, AC9E4LY05

Imaginative text – Folktale

How the Shark got its Bump

A popular story from the Cook Islands is about Ina and the shark.

A long time ago, there lived a beautiful girl named Ina. She loved a boy named Tinirau, but he lived on a distant island. Ina decided to swim to him. After swimming for a long time, Ina became tired. Then she saw a huge shark.

"Great shark," she said, "you are big and strong. Please take me to my beloved Tinirau."

The shark agreed to carry her on his back.

Ina had brought some coconuts with her for the journey. After a while, she called out, "I am thirsty, great shark. I have coconuts, but I can't open them."

"You may crack a coconut on my dorsal fin, but be careful," said the shark.

So, Ina cracked the coconut and drank the delicious milk. After a while, Ina grew thirsty again. This time, she cracked the coconut on the shark's head without asking him. At once, the shark tossed her off his back. He was about to eat her, when Tekea the Great, king of all sharks, rose from the sea.

"Jump on my back," said Tekea to Ina. "I will take you to Tinirau's island, but you must leave my sharks alone."

And to this day, the bump on the top of a shark's head is called Ina's bump.

Source: Text and image from *Rhythm and Dance, Polynesian Culture* by Rita Faelli, Blake Education.

TARGETING ENGLISH HOMEWORK YEAR 4 © PASCAL PRESS ISBN 978 1 925726 61 9

Reading & Comprehension

Shade the bubble next to the correct answer.

1. Where is this story from?
   - ◯ Australia
   - ◯ the Cook Islands
   - ◯ Britain

2. Who is the main character?
   - ◯ Ina
   - ◯ Tinirau
   - ◯ Tekea

3. Why did Ina ask the shark to carry her?
   - ◯ She thought it would be fun.
   - ◯ She couldn't swim.
   - ◯ She was tired.

4. Why did Ina want to go to a distant island?
   - ◯ She didn't like her island.
   - ◯ Her friend lived there.
   - ◯ She wanted to ride on a shark.

5. What did Ina take with her for the journey?
   - ◯ coconuts
   - ◯ milk
   - ◯ healthy snacks

6. How did Ina open the first coconut?
   - ◯ on the shark's head
   - ◯ on the shark's dorsal fin
   - ◯ on the shark's tail

7. How did Ina open the second coconut?
   - ◯ on the shark's head
   - ◯ on the shark's dorsal fin
   - ◯ on the shark's tail

8. Why did the shark toss Ina into the water?
   - ◯ He wanted to eat her.
   - ◯ She hadn't asked permission to crack the coconut on his head.
   - ◯ He was tired from carrying her.

9. What did Tekea tell Ina she would have to do?
   - ◯ stay on Tinirau's island
   - ◯ not eat any more coconuts
   - ◯ leave the sharks alone

10. Why is the bump on a shark's head called Ina's bump?
    - ◯ because Ina cracked a coconut on the shark's head
    - ◯ because Ina rode on a shark
    - ◯ because Tekea liked Ina and thought it was a good name

TERM 3

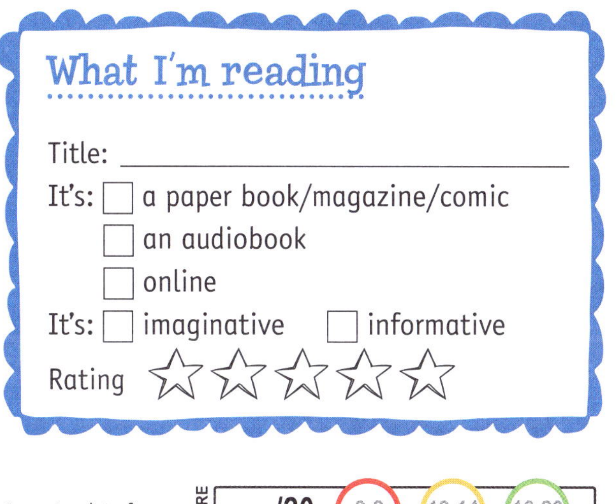

Score 2 points for each correct answer!

SCORE /20  

Grammar & Punctuation

AC9E4LA06, AC9E4LA08, AC9E4LY06

Simple, compound and complex sentences

Remember! A clause is a group of words with one subject and one verb.

A simple sentence consists of one independent clause.

A compound sentence is made up of two or more independent clauses joined by conjunctions.

A complex sentence is made up of one main independent clause, also called the principal clause, and one or more dependent clauses.

Circle the verbs or verb groups in these sentences. Underline the main clause. Write S for a simple sentence, C for a compound sentence and X for a complex sentence.

1. _____ A long time ago, there lived a beautiful girl named Ina.
2. _____ She loved a boy named Tinirau, but he lived on a distant island.
3. _____ Ina decided to swim to him.
4. _____ Ina had coconuts with her, but she couldn't open them.
5. _____ The shark was about to eat Ina when the king of all sharks rose from the sea.
6. _____ I will take you to Tinirau's island, but you must leave my sharks alone.
7. _____ Ina got thirsty while she was riding on the shark's back.
8. _____ It would be a long time before Ina got to Tinirau's island.
9. _____ To this day, the bump on the top of a shark's head is called Ina's bump.
10. ____ Ina cracked the coconut and drank the delicious milk.

Adverbial phrases and prepositions

Remember! Adverbial phrases tell how, where, when and why things happen.

They often begin with a preposition.

Highlight the verb and underline the adverbial phrase in each sentence. Circle the preposition if there is one. Write what the adverbial phrase tells about the verb: H (how), T (time/when), P (place/where) or W (why).

11. _____ A long time ago, there lived a beautiful girl named Ina.
12. _____ Tinirau lived on a distant island.
13. _____ She decided to swim to him.
14. _____ After swimming for a long time, Ina became tired.
15. _____ Ina took some coconuts for the journey.
16. _____ Ina cracked a coconut on the shark's dorsal fin.
17. _____ The shark tossed her off his back.
18. _____ Tekea the Great saved Ina from the shark.
19. _____ The shark carried Ina on his back.
20. _____ The bump on the top of a shark's head is called Ina's bump.

Adverbial clauses

Like adverbial phrases, adverbial clauses tell how, where, when and why things happen. They are joined to the principal clause by a conjunction. They are found in complex sentences.

Circle the verbs or verb groups in these complex sentences. Underline the adverbial clauses. Write what the adverbial clause tells about the main clause: H, T, P or W.

21. _____ Ina decided to swim to him because he lived on a distant island.
22. _____ After Ina had been swimming for a long time, she was very tired.
23. _____ He was about to eat her when Tekea the Great rose out of the sea.
24. _____ Because she hadn't asked, the shark tossed her off his back.

Score 2 points for each correct answer!

SCORE	/48	0-22	24-42	44-48

TERM 3

TARGETING ENGLISH HOMEWORK YEAR 4 © PASCAL PRESS ISBN 978 1 925726 61 9

AC9E4LY09, AC9E4LY11

The suffix 'ful'

The suffix 'ful' is added to a word to make a new word. It generally means 'full of'.

Example: beautiful = full of beauty
Adjective: a beautiful flower

It may also mean 'tending to' or 'able to'.

Example: harmful = able to harm
Adjective: a harmful snake

Sometimes it means 'able to fill'.

Example: spoonful = filling a spoon
Noun: a spoonful of sugar

Add the suffix 'ful' to each of these words to make a new word.

1. beauty ______________________
2. care ______________________
3. flavour ______________________
4. cheer ______________________
5. skill ______________________
6. peace ______________________
7. cup ______________________
8. doubt ______________________
9. mind ______________________
10. wonder ______________________

Choose 'ful' words from 1 – 10 to complete these sentences.

11. Ina's coconut milk was very ______________________.
12. The shark was ______________________ as he carried Ina towards the island.
13. It is ______________________ whether Ina has learned her lesson.
14. It would be ______________________ to ride on a shark's back like Ina did.
15. Ina needs to learn to be ______________________ of other's feelings.

Apostrophes – Contractions and possession

Apostrophes are used in contractions. Contractions are two words shortened into one word. They are often used in speaking.

Examples:

"**I'm** thirsty," said Ina.
("**I am** thirsty," said Ina.)

"I **can't** open them."
("I **cannot** open them.")

Apostrophes are also used to show possession or ownership.

Examples:
shark**'s** head Tinirau**'s** island Ina**'s** bump

Watch out! Don't confuse it's and its.

It's is a contraction. It means 'it is' or 'it has'.

Examples: **It's** the first day of the holidays.
(**It is** the first day of the holidays.)

Its is a possessive pronoun. It is used to show possession.

Example: The cat licked **its** paw.
(its own paw, not it is paw)

Read these sentences. Circle the words with an apostrophe. Write C for contraction. Write P for possession.

16. _____ Ina couldn't open the coconuts.
17. _____ Ina cracked the coconut on the shark's head.
18. _____ Tekea took Ina to Tinirau's island.
19. _____ "You're very big and strong," Ina said to the shark.
20. _____ "I'll take you to the island," said Tekea.
21. _____ "You mustn't do that again," said Tekea.
22. _____ Ina's action was hurtful to the shark.

Write the contractions from exercises 16 – 22 and the two words that were shortened.

23. ______________ = __________ + __________
24. ______________ = __________ + __________
25. ______________ = __________ + __________
26. ______________ = __________ + __________

Score 2 points for each correct answer! SCORE /52 0-24 26-46 48-52

TERM 3

AC9E4LA03, AC9E4LY03, AC9E4LY04, AC9E4LY05, AC9HS4K01, AC9HS4K02, AC9HS4K04, AC9HS4S03

Informative text – Timeline

History of People in Australia

More than 45 000 years ago	Rock engravings in South Australia show that the land was inhabited.
Mid 1400s	First Nations Australians are trading with people from Indonesia.
1606	Dutchman, William Jansz, explores the coast of Cape York. It is the first European contact with First Nations Australians.
1770	Englishman, James Cook, claims the whole east coast of Australia for Great Britain.
1788	The First Fleet lands in Port Jackson. British colonisation of Australia begins. First Nations Australians resist the takeover of their land.
1828	The Black Wars in Tasmania begin. Tasmanian Aboriginals are later taken to Flinders Island.
1836 - 1837	The British Parliament says that Aboriginal people have a "plain right and sacred right" to their land. It recommends that Protectors of Aborigines are appointed in Australia.
1869	The Governor of Victoria gets the power to remove any Aboriginal child from their family.
1881	The Protector of Aborigines in NSW has the power to create reserves and to force Aboriginal people to live on them.
1890	Jandamarra, an Aboriginal resistance fighter, declares war on settlers in the West Kimberley, Western Australia.
1901	Australia becomes a Federation. The Constitution states that Aboriginal people will not be counted in the census.
1969	Laws end that allow removal of Aboriginal children from their families.
1976	The Australian Government recognises Aboriginal land ownership. Aboriginal people can claim recognition of their lands.
1992	The High Court decides on the "Mabo" case. It rules that native title can exist and that Australia was never an "empty land".
2008	The Prime Minister apologises to the Stolen Generations on behalf of the Australian Government.

Source: Text adapted from *First Australians* by Carolyn Tate, a Go Facts book, Blake Education.

TERM 3

TARGETING ENGLISH HOMEWORK YEAR 4 © PASCAL PRESS ISBN 978 1 925726 61 9

Reading & Comprehension

Shade the bubble next to the correct answer.

1. How do we know that Australia was inhabited more than 45 000 years ago?
   - ◯ Rock engravings in South Australia are that old.
   - ◯ Somebody said 45 000 years and it seems like a good idea.
   - ◯ People told Captain Cook when he visited Australia in 1770.

2. Who did First Nations Australians trade with in the mid-1400s?
   - ◯ Captain Cook
   - ◯ Britain
   - ◯ People from Indonesia

3. Who was the first European to have contact with First Nations Australians?
   - ◯ Captain Cook
   - ◯ William Jansz
   - ◯ People from Indonesia

4. Did First Nations Australians welcome the First Fleet in 1788?
   - ◯ Yes. They were pleased to have visitors.
   - ◯ No. They resisted the takeover of their land.
   - ◯ Unsure.

5. Were interactions between First Nations Australians and the colonists always peaceful?
   - ◯ Yes. First Nations Australians welcomed the colonists onto their land.
   - ◯ No. There were wars as some First Nations Australians resisted the takeover of their land.
   - ◯ Unsure.

6. In what year did the Governor of Victoria get the power to remove any Aboriginal child from their family?
   - ◯ 1770
   - ◯ 1869
   - ◯ 1901

7. What year saw the end of the law allowing Aboriginal children to be removed from their families?
   - ◯ 1869
   - ◯ 1881
   - ◯ 1969

8. When did the Australian Government recognise Aboriginal land ownership?
   - ◯ 1770
   - ◯ 1901
   - ◯ 1976

9. What did the High Court decide in the "Mabo" case in 1992?
   - ◯ Australia was never an "empty land".
   - ◯ First Nations Australian should be counted in the census.
   - ◯ Aboriginal children should not be taken from their families.

10. What did the Prime Minister say to the Stolen Generations in 2008?
    - ◯ "We forgive you."
    - ◯ "Sorry."
    - ◯ "Let's forget the past."

TERM 3

What I'm reading

Title: ______________________

It's: ☐ a paper book/magazine/comic
☐ an audiobook
☐ online

It's: ☐ imaginative ☐ informative

Rating ☆ ☆ ☆ ☆ ☆

Score 2 points for each correct answer!

SCORE /20 0-8 10-14 16-20

Grammar & Punctuation

AC9E4LA09, AC9E4LA11, AC9E4LA12, AC9E4LY06

Verb tense – Adding 'ed' and 'ing'

Remember! For most verbs, when we change tense to past or present continuous, we simply add 'ed' or 'ing' to the base verb.

Example: show showed showing

When the base verb ends with 'e', we leave off the 'e' and add 'ed' or 'ing'.

Example: explore explored exploring

When the base verb has one vowel followed by one consonant, we double the consonant before adding 'ed' and 'ing'.

Example: stop stopped stopping

Some verbs don't follow the usual pattern for past tense. Instead of adding 'ed', the verb changes.

Example: Today I **think**. I am **thinking**.
Yesterday I **thought**.

Write the past and present continuous forms of these verbs.

	Base verb	Past tense	Present continuous
1	trade		
2	claim		
3	begin		
4	say		
5	allow		

Historical present tense

In some historical documents, such as the timeline on page 78, writers use present tense to give the impression you are moving through time alongside the events as they occur. It is called the historical present tense.

Circle the present tense verbs in these sentences, then rewrite the sentences in past tense to show that the events have already occurred.

6. Rock engravings in South Australia show that the land was inhabited.

7. The First Fleet lands in Port Jackson.

8. Australia becomes a Federation.

9. The Australian Government recognises Aboriginal land ownership.

10. The Prime Minister apologises to the Stolen Generations.

Proper nouns

Remember! Proper nouns are the names of particular people, places, objects and events. Proper nouns begin with a capital letter.

Sort proper nouns from the timeline on page 78 into this table. Remember to use capital letters.

People	Places
11	16
12	17
13	18
14	19
15	20

Objects	Events
21	26
22	27
23	28
24	29
25	30

Score 2 points for each correct answer! SCORE /60

TERM 3

TARGETING ENGLISH HOMEWORK YEAR 4 © PASCAL PRESS ISBN 978 1 925726 61 9

Phonic & Word Knowledge

UNIT 18

AC9E4LY09, AC9E4LY10

Suffixes 'ion', 'tion' and 'ation'

The suffixes '-ion', '-tion' and '-ation' are used to change verbs into nouns. The suffixes are pronounced 'shun' with the schwa sound or 'ashun' with the 'long a' vowel sound and the schwa sound.

If verbs end with 'ate' or 'pt', we add '-ion'.

Examples:
federate federat**ion** adopt adopt**ion**

(Notice we drop the 'e' in federate.)

If the verb ends with 'ne', 've' or 're', we drop the 'e' then add '-ation'.

If it ends with a consonant, we also add '-ation'.

Examples: reserve reserv**ation**
recommend recommend**ation**

Draw lines to match nouns with the verbs they are built from.

1 constitution	**a** reserve
2 recommendation	**b** protect
3 recognition	**c** colonise
4 decision	**d** federate
5 reservation	**e** communicate
6 protection	**f** recommend
7 federation	**g** recognise
8 colonisation	**h** decide
9 communication	**i** educate
10 education	**j** constitute

Syllables

Break these words into syllables. For each word, write the number of syllables, then show the syllables separated by a + sign.

11 _____ constitution ____________________
12 _____ federation ____________________
13 _____ protection ____________________
14 _____ communication ____________________
15 _____ colonisation ____________________
16 _____ decision ____________________

Suffixes 'er', 'or' and 'ar'

The suffixes '-er', '-or' and '-ar' are used to change verbs into nouns, meaning a person or a thing that does the verb.

Example: A teach**er** is one who teaches.

The suffixes all sound the same, but '-er' is used most often.

The rules for adding these suffixes are similar to those for adding other suffixes, for example, drop the 'e' or double the final consonant.

Use the suffix '-er' to write the words with the following meanings.

17 One who explores is an ____________________.
18 One who trades is a ____________________.
19 One who colonises is a ____________________.
20 One who resists is a ____________________.

Use the suffix '-or' to write the words with the following meanings.

21 One who governs is a ____________________.
22 One who protects is a ____________________.
23 One who survives is a ____________________.
24 One who supervises is a ____________________.

Score 2 points for each correct answer!

SCORE /48  0-22  24-42  44-48 

TERM 3

Imaginative text – A play

The Dragon Slayer

The story so far: Prince Fretalot, the Prince of Grumbleton, has been sent by his wife, Princess Complainia, to slay the dragon which set fire to their village.

Setting:	**The Dragon's valley**
Characters:	**Narrator, Prince Fretalot, Dragon, Sir Shmelly, Sir Hardbottom, Sir Blunt**
Narrator:	The prince and his knights finally arrive in the Dragon's valley. They discover a dragon sitting and roasting pumpkins over a flame.
Prince Fretalot:	Dragon, prepare to meet your doom.
Dragon:	Oh, is my father coming? He doesn't like me very much. You see, I've become a vegetarian, which rather goes against dragon lore. I really love pumpkin soup. Would you like some? It's my own special recipe.
Prince Fretalot:	What? No! Sir Shmelly, be ready to unleash your worst.
Sir Shmelly:	Yes, sire!
Dragon:	Now, hold on a minute. What seems to be the problem? Let's talk about this.
Sir Hardbottom:	Be silent, worm! Your days of mayhem are over.
Dragon:	Mayhem? Worm? Steady on, I happen to be a dragon and I only took a couple of pumpkins.
Sir Blunt:	Pumpkins? Aren't you the dragon that set fire to the village?
Dragon:	No, that was my father. Now, are you going to have some soup or not?
Prince Fretalot:	Err ...
Sir Shmelly:	It does smell delicious.
Sir Hardbottom:	And it would be a shame to waste all those pumpkins.
Narrator:	And so the prince and the knights made friends with the dragon, ate delicious pumpkin soup and returned home without slaying anything.

Source: Text from *How to Make a Princess Happy* by Elizabeth Klein in Australian Readers' Theatre Middle Primary, Blake Education.

TERM 3

Reading & Comprehension

Write your answers on the lines provided.

1. What is the title of the play?

2. Where does the story take place?

3. Who is the main character in the play?

4. What is the main character's task? Why?

5. Which other characters support or help the main character?

6. Does the main character achieve their goal? Explain.

7. Why doesn't the dragon's father like him?

8. What did the dragon do that was wrong?

9. How did the dragon convince the knights to not kill him?

10. Do you think the knights will return to visit the dragon? Explain.

TERM 3

What I'm reading

Title: ____________________

It's: ☐ a paper book/magazine/comic
☐ an audiobook
☐ online

It's: ☐ imaginative ☐ informative

Rating ☆ ☆ ☆ ☆ ☆

Score 2 points for each correct answer!

SCORE /20 0-8 10-14 16-20

Grammar & Punctuation

AC9E4LA07, AC9E4LA11, AC9E4LA12, AC9E4LE04, AC9E4LY06

Direct speech

Remember! Writers usually use speech marks or quotation marks ("…") to identify the words spoken by characters. They use saying verbs to show who is talking and how.

In a play, writers record the actual words spoken by each character, but do not use quotation marks or saying verbs.

Rewrite these sections of dialogue from the play as direct speech. Remember to punctuate the sentences correctly and use appropriate saying verbs.

1. **Prince Fretalot: Dragon, prepare to meet your doom.**

   ____

2. **Dragon: Now, hold on a minute. What seems to be the problem?**

   ____

3. **Sir Blunt: Aren't you the dragon that set fire to the village?**

   ____

4. **Sir Shmelly: It does smell delicious.**

   ____

5. **Sir Hardbottom: Be silent, worm! Your days of mayhem are over.**

   ____

Indirect speech

Reported or indirect speech is reported by another person. It is reported in the past tense and gives the gist of what was said rather than the actual words. Quotation marks are not used.

Example: The dragon said that he hadn't set the village on fire. He said it was his father.

Rewrite these sections of dialogue from the play as indirect speech. Remember to use appropriate saying verbs but quotation marks are not needed.

6. **Prince Fretalot: Sir Shmelly, be ready to unleash your worst.**

   ____

7. **Dragon: My father doesn't like me much. I've become a vegetarian.**

   ____

8. **Sir Blunt: Aren't you the dragon that set fire to the village?**

   ____

9. **Sir Shmelly: It does smell delicious.**

   ____

10. **Sir Hardbottom: It would be a shame to waste all those pumpkins.**

    ____

TERM 3

Synonyms

Synonyms are words with similar meanings. A synonym for large is big.

Write synonyms for these words from the play.

11. slay ______________________
12. roasting ______________________
13. recipe ______________________
14. unleash ______________________
15. lore ______________________
16. problem ______________________

Antonyms

Antonyms are words with opposite meanings. An antonym for large is small.

Write antonyms for these words from the play.

17. slay ______________________
18. complain ______________________
19. coming ______________________
20. mayhem ______________________
21. friends ______________________
22. delicious ______________________

Score 2 points for each correct answer!

SCORE /44   

TARGETING ENGLISH HOMEWORK YEAR 4 © PASCAL PRESS ISBN 978 1 925726 61 9

Phonic & Word Knowledge

UNIT 19

AC9E4LE04, AC9E4LY10, AC9E4LY11

Word meanings

The writer has used names to help identify the characters' personalities and behaviours. Draw lines to match characters to their personality traits.

1. Prince Fretalot
2. Prince of Grumbleton
3. Princess Complainia
4. Sir Shmelly
5. Sir Hardbottom
6. Sir Blunt

a never happy, always whinging

b worried and anxious

c straight-talking, doesn't care about others' feelings

d difficult to get along with, ready to fight

e constantly groaning and moaning

f needs to take a bath more often

Plurals

Remember! To make a word plural (more than one), you usually just add -s.

For words that end in ch, sh, s, ss, x, z or zz, you add -es to make them plural.

For words that end in y, you change the y to i and add -es, as in fairies; but not if it ends in ey, as in monkeys, ay as in days, or oy as in boys.

However, you need to be careful of words that don't follow the rules, like oxen and sheep.

Write the plural for these words.

7. prince ______________________
8. princess ______________________
9. knight ______________________
10. flame ______________________
11. grass ______________________
12. valley ______________________
13. pumpkin ______________________
14. fish ______________________
15. lady ______________________
16. dragon ______________________

Apostrophes – Contractions and possession

Read these sentences. Circle the words with an apostrophe. Write C for contraction. Write P for possession.

17. _____ The knights arrive at the Dragon's valley.
18. _____ Let's talk about this.
19. _____ Aren't you the dragon that set fire to the village?
20. _____ The dragon's father didn't like him because he was a vegetarian.

Write the two words that these contractions are made from.

21. let's = ____________ + ____________
22. I'll = ____________ + ____________
23. don't = ____________ + ____________
24. doesn't = ____________ + ____________
25. you're = ____________ + ____________
26. they've = ____________ + ____________

Silent letters 'g' and 'k'

When the letters 'g' and 'k' occur before the letter 'n' at the beginning of a word, they are usually silent.

Examples: gnome knight

Draw lines to match the words and the pictures.

27. 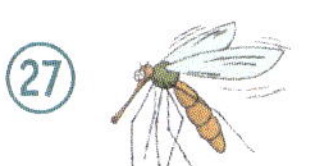
28. 
29. 
30. 
31. 
32. 
33. 
34. 

gnome

gnu

gnat

knot

knight

knitting

knife

knee

Homophones

Choose the correct word to complete each sentence.

35. The moon was shining bright that ____________. (knight, night)
36. Sir Hardbottom wanted to have ____________ pumpkin soup. (some, sum)
37. The dragon said he did ____________ start the fire in the village. (knot, not)
38. The knights did not ____________ how good the soup would be. (know, no)

Score 2 points for each correct answer! SCORE /76   

TERM 3

AC9E4LA03, AC9E4LY03, AC9E4LY04, AC9E4LY05

Persuasive text – Opinion

What Makes a Good Teacher?

We are always being told what we have to do to be a good student.

Listen in class. Put up your hand to speak. Be polite. Follow the rules. It's always the teachers telling us kids what to do. I think it's about time we told the teachers what they need to do to be good teachers. A lot of them don't seem to know what it takes.

First, a good teacher always likes kids. Grumpy teachers who don't like kids never make good teachers.

A good teacher has to be kind to kids, always, but especially when they are hurt or upset.

A good teacher listens to kids and respects their opinions.

A good teacher has a sense of humour. A good teacher likes to laugh and tell jokes but never makes fun of kids.

A good teacher is patient and does not get cross every time a kid makes a mistake, like getting a sum wrong or forgetting to put up their hand.

I think every teacher should be a good teacher. If I was going to write a report for my teacher, I'd give her an A+ for everything.

TARGETING ENGLISH HOMEWORK YEAR 4 © PASCAL PRESS ISBN 978 1 925726 61 9

Reading & Comprehension

Shade the bubble next to the correct answer. Write the answer on the line where appropriate.

1. Who is the writer of this opinion piece?
   - ◯ a student
   - ◯ a teacher
   - ◯ a parent

2. What is the main idea of the article?
   - ◯ Students should follow the rules in class.
   - ◯ Teachers should be reported.
   - ◯ How teachers should treat students.

3. Which of these are children **not** told to do?
   - ◯ listen in class
   - ◯ put up their hands to speak
   - ◯ report the teacher

4. Why does the writer think it's time to tell the teachers what to do?
   - ◯ They are tired of teachers telling students what to do.
   - ◯ Many teachers don't know how to be good teachers.
   - ◯ It's not fair if teachers can tell students what to do, and students can't tell teachers what to do.

5. What types of teachers does the writer **not** like?
   - ◯ grumpy teachers
   - ◯ teachers with a sense of humour
   - ◯ patient teachers
   - ◯ kind teachers

6. According to the writer, what makes a good teacher?
   - ◯ someone who is patient and kind
   - ◯ someone who gets cross at kids when they make a mistake
   - ◯ someone who laughs at kids
   - ◯ someone who gives kids an A+ for everything

7. Is the writer's teacher a good teacher?
   - ◯ Yes
   - ◯ No

   How do you know? ______________________

   ____

   ____

8. Do you agree with the writer about what makes a good teacher?
   - ◯ Yes
   - ◯ No
   - ◯ Unsure

   Explain: ______________________

   ____

   ____

9. What do you know about the writer's teacher?
   - ◯ They are young.
   - ◯ They are old.
   - ◯ They are patient and kind.
   - ◯ They don't tell the children what to do.

10. In what ways is your teacher a good teacher?

    ____

    ____

    ____

    ____

    ____

    ____

TERM 3

What I'm reading

Title: ______________________

It's: ☐ a paper book/magazine/comic
☐ an audiobook
☐ online

It's: ☐ imaginative ☐ informative

Rating ☆ ☆ ☆ ☆ ☆

Score 2 points for each correct answer! SCORE /20

Grammar & Punctuation

AC9E4LA02, AC9E4LA06, AC9E4LA11, AC9E4LY06

Emotive words

In an article expressing an opinion, emotive words are used to convince the reader to feel the same way as the writer does.

Examples: always, never, especially, should

Circle the emotive words in each of these sentences. There may be more than one.

1. We are always being told what we have to do to be a good student.
2. I think it's about time we told the teachers what they need to do to be good teachers.
3. A good teacher has to be kind to kids, always, but especially when they are hurt or upset.
4. But a good teacher never makes fun of kids.
5. A good teacher is patient and does not get cross every time a kid makes a mistake.

Thinking and feeling verbs

When we write or talk about our thoughts and feelings, we can use certain words to express our opinion.

Examples: I think   I believe   I feel
In my opinion   My favourite
It seems to me   I tend to think   The best

Choose a suitable phrase from above to complete these sentences.

6. ______________ that students deserve good teachers.
7. My teacher is ______________ and I would give her an A+.
8. ______________ that children don't do good work if they are scared.
9. It may sound funny, but ______________ teachers need a sense of humour.
10. You might disagree with me, but ______________ chocolate is the best!

Adjectives

Remember! Adjectives are words used to describe people, places and things. They tell more about a noun.

Example: a **good** teacher

The article describes qualities considered important for being a good teacher. List three adjectives used to describe a good teacher. Then list their antonyms (opposites).

A good teacher is:	is not:
11. ______________	14. ______________
12. ______________	15. ______________
13. ______________	16. ______________

Adjectival clauses

In a complex sentence, subordinate clauses may do the work of adjectives. They might tell us more about nouns. Adjectival clauses always follow the nouns they describe. They are linked to the principal clause by the relative pronouns: who, whom, which, that.

Examples: Mrs Smith is a good teacher **who** likes to tell jokes.
The report **that** I wrote for my teacher is a good one.

Underline the adjectival clauses in these sentences. Circle the relative pronouns. Highlight the nouns that the adjectival clauses describe.

17. Grumpy teachers who don't like kids never make good teachers.
18. A good teacher never gets cross with a kid who makes a mistake.
19. It's always the teachers who tell kids what to do.
20. I wrote a report that gave my teacher an A+.

Score 2 points for each correct answer!

SCORE  /40  0-18  20-34  36-40

TERM 3

TARGETING ENGLISH HOMEWORK YEAR 4 © PASCAL PRESS ISBN 978 1 925726 61 9

AC9E4LY09, AC9E4LY10

The digraph 'sh' and the sound 'sh'

The digraph 'sh' is usually used to represent the sound 'sh' as in ship and shoe. But there are many other ways of spelling the 'sh' sound too.

Say each word in the word bank. They each have the sound 'sh' in them.

should	na**t**ion	federa**t**ion	pa**t**ient
espe**c**ially	**sh**irt	**s**ugar	**ch**ute
ac**t**ion	i**ss**ue	o**c**ean	man**s**ion
schwa	spe**c**ial	an**x**ious	

Choose words from the word bank to complete these sentences.

1. A good teacher is always ________________.
2. I like to have ________________ on my cereal for breakfast.
3. Dwayne "The Rock" Johnson is an ________________ hero.
4. A teacher should be kind, ________________ when kids are hurt or upset.
5. The children love to take their boogie boards to surf in the ________________.
6. The billionaire lives in a ________________ at the top of the hill.
7. The boy used to chew his nails when he was ________________, but now he doesn't.
8. All the children in the choir needed to wear a white ________________.

The digraph 'gh'

Remember! The letter 'g' is used to represent the 'hard g' sound. *Example:* good

It is also used to represent the 'soft g' sound or 'j' sound. *Example:* gem

When it is part of a digraph with the letter 'h', it represents different sounds.

At the beginning of a word, the digraph 'gh' usually represents the 'hard g' sound. *Example:* **gh**ost

When it is at the end of a word, it sometimes makes the 'f' sound. *Example:* lau**gh**

Sometimes, in the middle or at the end of a word, it is silent or helps to spell the vowel sound. *Examples:* hi**gh**, cau**gh**t

Say each word in the word bank. They each have the digraph 'gh' in them.

hi**gh**	**gh**ost	lau**gh**	nau**gh**ty
ei**gh**t	**gh**oul	enou**gh**	si**gh**
slei**gh**	**gh**astly	cou**gh**	tou**gh**
ghetto	**Gh**ana	rou**gh**	

Sort the words in the word bank into the table.

'hard g'
9
10
11
12
13
'f'
14
15
16
17
18
silent
19
20
21
22
23

The diagraph 'ng'

The letter 'g' also combines with the letter 'n' to form the digraph 'ng'. There are six different words with the digraph 'ng' in the text. Can you find four of them?

24. ________________
25. ________________
26. ________________
27. ________________

Score 2 points for each correct answer!

SCORE /54

TERM 3

AC9E4LA03, AC9E4LY03, AC9E4LY04, AC9E4LY05, AC9HS4K01, AC9HS4K05, AC9HS4K07, AC9HS4K09

Informative text – Report

Dreaming Stories

Dreaming stories are the stories of First Nations Australians. They are stories told by the Elders to younger members of their community.

Dreaming stories explain:

1. how and why the world is the way it is
2. why birds, animals and people appear and behave the way they do
3. how natural features such as stars, mountains and other landforms came to exist where they are today
4. how people should behave towards each other and what happens when people do not follow the rules.

First Nations Australians have been living in Australia for tens of thousands of years. Their culture is diverse. Many communities have their own language and their own Dreaming stories. Their stories were never written down. They were told through stories, dance and art.

Dreaming stories show the important link between First Nations Australian people and the land. First Nations Australians believe that they came from the land, and they believe that they need to look after it. It is their past, their present and their future. It gives them their spiritual identity as well as food and shelter.

Dreaming stories are not 'owned' by any one person. They belong to the entire community of First Nations Australians.

Source: Text adapted from *Targeting Text Interactively, Middle Dreaming Legend*, Blake Education.

TERM 3

Shade the bubble next to the correct answer. Write the answers on the line where appropriate.

1. What are Dreaming stories?
   - ◯ stories we tell about our dreams
   - ◯ stories told by First Nations Australians
   - ◯ stories caught in dream catchers

2. Who tells Dreaming stories?
   - ◯ First Nations Australian Elders
   - ◯ First Nations Australian young people
   - ◯ any storytellers

3. How long have Dreaming stories been told?
   - ◯ since Europeans came to Australia
   - ◯ for ten years
   - ◯ for thousands of years

4. What do Dreaming stories **not** explain?
   - ◯ why the world is the way it is
   - ◯ why birds, animals and people behave the way they do
   - ◯ why Europeans came to Australia
   - ◯ what should happen if people don't follow the rules

5. What are **natural features** explained by Dreaming stories?
   - ◯ stars, mountains, rivers
   - ◯ boomerangs and clapping sticks
   - ◯ birds and animals

6. How were Dreaming stories passed down from generation to generation?
   - ◯ in books
   - ◯ over the internet
   - ◯ through stories, dance and art

7. What important **link** do Dreaming stories show?
   - ◯ between First Nations Australians and the land
   - ◯ between First Nations Australians and the birds and animals
   - ◯ between First Nations Australians and the European arrivals

8. Why is the land important to First Nations Australians?
   - ◯ They need somewhere to live.
   - ◯ It gives them their spirituality as well as food and shelter.
   - ◯ They were here first.

9. Are Dreaming stories the same all over Australia?
   - ◯ Yes
   - ◯ No
   - ◯ Unsure

   Explain: ______________________________

   ____

   ____

   ____

   ____

10. Write the title of a Dreaming story you know. What does it explain?

    ____

    ____

    ____

    ____

    ____

    ____

    ____

    ____

Score 2 points for each correct answer!

SCORE /20

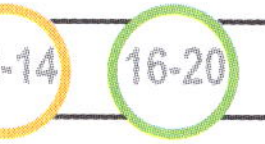

TERM 3

AC9E4LA06, AC9E4LA08, AC9E4LA12, AC9E4LY06

Bullet points and sentences

Bullet points are used in lists. Each item in a bullet point may be a word, a phrase, a clause or a sentence. The items may be organised under an introductory word, phrase, clause or sentence.

In the *Dreaming Stories* article, the items are introduced by a clause. Each bullet point concludes the sentence with a clause telling what the Dreaming stories explain.

Example: Dreaming stories explain how and why the world is the way it is.

Use information in the text to write clauses to conclude each sentence.

1. Dreaming stories explain ______________________

2. Dreaming stories explain ______________________

3. Dreaming stories explain ______________________

Write the information in these sentences as bullet points. Rember to write an introductory word, phrase, clause or sentence.

Dreaming stories have been told for tens of thousands of years. They were never written down. They were told through stories, dance, and art. Dreaming stories belong to the entire community of First Nations Australians.

4. ______________________

5. ______________________

6. ______________________

7. ______________________

8. ______________________

Adverbial phrases and clauses

Remember! Adverbial phrases tell how, where, when and why things happen.

They often begin with a preposition. They do not have a verb.

Example: Dreaming stories (have been told) <u>for thousands of years</u>.

Like adverbial phrases, adverbial clauses tell how, where, when and why things happen.

They are found in complex sentences, and they do have a verb. They are joined to the principal clause by a conjunction.

Example: Dreaming stories (are) important <u>because they (link) First Nations Australian people and the land</u>.

Circle the verbs in these sentences. Underline the adverbial phrases and adverbial clauses that give more information about the verb. Highlight the preposition or conjunction. Write P for an adverbial phrase. Write C for an adverbial clause.

9. ____ Dreaming stories are told through stories, dance and art.

10. _____ Dreaming stories are told by the Elders to younger members of their communities.

11. _____ Dreaming stories are diverse because there are many different communities of First Nations Australians.

12. _____ Dreaming stories tell what happens when people don't follow the rules.

Score 2 points for each correct answer! SCORE /24 0-10 12-18 20-24

TERM 3

TARGETING ENGLISH HOMEWORK YEAR 4 © PASCAL PRESS ISBN 978 1 925726 61 9

Phonic & Word Knowledge

UNIT 21

AC9E4LY09, AC9E4LY10

Plurals

When making nouns plural, remember the rules for adding 's' and 'es' or changing the 'y' to 'i' before adding 'es'.

Examples: stick – stick**s** gas – gas**es**
story – stor**ies**

Look out for words that don't follow the rules.

Write the plural for these words.

1. Australian ______
2. person ______
3. animal ______
4. story ______
5. thousand ______
6. identity ______
7. class ______
8. star ______
9. rule ______
10. community ______

The sounds 's' and 'z'

The letter 's' usually represents the 's' sound that we hear at the beginning of **s**tory.

The letter 'z' usually represents the 'z' sound that we hear at the beginning of **z**oo.

But often, the letter 's' that makes a word plural is pronounced 'z' as in bird**s**.

Say these words. Look at the letters in bold type. Write S if you hear the 's' sound and Z if you hear the 'z' sound.

11. ______ exi**s**t
12. ______ mountain**s**
13. ______ **s**tory
14. ______ storie**s**
15. ______ pre**s**ent
16. ______ rule**s**
17. ______ elder**s**
18. ______ fir**s**t
19. ______ diver**s**e

Compound words

Write the word land before each of these words to make a compound word.

20. ______forms
21. ______fill
22. ______fall
23. ______mark
24. ______owner
25. ______slide
26. ______scape
27. ______mass
28. ______ward
29. ______lord

Choose a compound word from examples 20 – 29 to complete these sentences.

30. Dreaming stories tell how mountains and other ______ came to exist.
31. There was a dangerous ______ on the hillside after continuous heavy rain.
32. The ______ was dotted with trees and small rocky outcrops.
33. The tired sailors hoped to make ______ before sunset.
34. The ______ kept increasing the rent and it became harder and harder to pay.
35. Uluru is a famous Australian ______ .

The vowel trigraph 'ure'

The vowel trigraph 'ure' often spells the sound 'your' as in p**ure** and c**ure**.

However, in words like nat**ure** and fut**ure**, it represents the schwa sound.

Say the words in the word bank. Sort them into the table.

rapture	cure	secure	culture
nurture	sure	insure	future

Rhymes with 'nature'	Rhymes with 'pure'
36.	40.
37.	41.
38.	42.
39.	43.

Score 2 points for each correct answer!

SCORE /86 0-40 42-80 82-86

TERM 3

AC9E4LA03, AC9E4LY03, AC9E4LY04, AC9E4LY05, AC9S4U03

Informative text – Report

Gravity

Have you ever heard the saying "What goes up must come down"? This is a true statement everywhere on Earth because of gravity. Gravity makes your feet hit the floor after you jump or a cricket ball fall into a player's glove. And it's the reason we stay on Earth's surface instead of floating off into space.

All objects with mass have gravity. The more mass an object has, the stronger its gravitational force will be on other objects. Earth's gravity is so powerful, it even keeps the moon in orbit around us!

Gravity doesn't just pull us down. It pulls us toward Earth's centre of mass. Because Earth is shaped like a sphere, its centre of mass is located in its core. Gravity pulls everything toward the centre of Earth in a straight line.

However, we can use force to stop an object from falling or to change its path. For example, when you catch a ball, you use force to stop gravity from pulling it all the way to the ground. When you swing on a swing, the seat stops you from falling.

In addition, the force of pumping your arms and legs makes you swing back and forth. Even when force stops an object from falling or changes its path, gravity is always pulling on it.

Source: Text and image adapted from *Targeting Science Year 4*, Pascal Press.

TARGETING ENGLISH HOMEWORK YEAR 4 © PASCAL PRESS ISBN 978 1 925726 61 9

Reading & Comprehension

Shade the bubble next to the correct answer.

1. What is this article mostly about?
   - ◯ playing cricket
   - ◯ jumping
   - ◯ gravity

2. What does gravity do? (Choose any that apply.)
   - ◯ keeps us on Earth's surface
   - ◯ pulls us towards the centre of the Earth
   - ◯ allows rockets to travel into space
   - ◯ makes everything fall back to Earth

3. What type of objects have gravity?
   - ◯ Earth
   - ◯ the moon
   - ◯ objects with mass

4. Which objects have **more** gravity?
   - ◯ round objects
   - ◯ objects in space
   - ◯ objects with more mass

5. Which of these has more gravity?
   - ◯ the Sun
   - ◯ Earth
   - ◯ the moon

6. What keeps the **moon** in orbit around Earth?
   - ◯ the Sun's gravity
   - ◯ Earth's gravity
   - ◯ the moon's gravity

7. Where is Earth's centre of mass?
   - ◯ at the equator
   - ◯ in the middle of the ocean
   - ◯ in its core

8. How does gravity pull things?
   - ◯ in a straight line
   - ◯ in a curved path
   - ◯ in a circle

9. What can be used to stop an object from falling?
   - ◯ your hand
   - ◯ force
   - ◯ a swing

10. Which of these is **not** affected by gravity?
    - ◯ a basketball
    - ◯ a rocket
    - ◯ the moon
    - ◯ a helium balloon
    - ◯ an orange
    - ◯ you
    - ◯ none of the above

TERM 3

What I'm reading

Title: ______________________

It's: ☐ a paper book/magazine/comic
☐ an audiobook
☐ online

It's: ☐ imaginative ☐ informative

Rating ☆ ☆ ☆ ☆ ☆

Score 2 points for each correct answer!

SCORE /20    

Grammar & Punctuation

AC9E4LA04, AC9E4LA06, AC9E4LA11, AC9E4LY06

Adverbial clauses

Remember! Adverbial clauses tell how, where, when and why things happen.

They are found in complex sentences and are joined to the principal clause by a conjunction. Adverbial clauses can be placed at the beginning of a sentence, in the middle or at the end.

Circle the verbs or verb groups in these sentences. Underline the adverbial clauses and highlight the conjunctions.

1. That is a true statement because gravity affects everything on Earth.
2. Gravity makes your feet hit the floor after you jump.
3. Although it may be smaller, an object with more mass has a stronger gravitational force.
4. Because Earth is shaped like a sphere, its centre of mass is located in its core.
5. When you swing on a swing, the seat stops you from falling.

Text connectives

Text connectives are words and phrases that join ideas together throughout the text.

They guide readers from one sentence to the next and one paragraph to the next. They are used to place information or events in order. They can be conjunctions, prepositions or adverbs.

Examples: although, however, therefore, consequently, because, later, until, then, so, as a result, meanwhile, afterwards, on the other hand, firstly, after lunch, later that day

Reread the text. Write the text connectives you find here.

6 – 10

____

____

____

____

____

TERM 3

Science topic words

Match these words to their meanings

11 gravity	a the amount of matter that an object contains
12 mass	b the force that pulls objects with mass together
13 force	c a pulling force that works across space
14 gravitational force	d the central part of an object
15 core	e a push or a pull on an object

Verb groups

A verb group has more than one verb. It is made up of a main verb and a helper verb.

Example: We **can use** force to stop an object from falling.

Circle the verb groups in these sentences.

16. The gravitational force will be stronger in objects with more mass.
17. The moon is orbiting around Earth.
18. You have heard the saying "What goes up must come down".
19. Earth's centre of mass is located in its core.
20. You can change the direction of a ball by using force.

Score 2 points for each correct answer! SCORE /40  0-18  20-34  36-40

TARGETING ENGLISH HOMEWORK YEAR 4 © PASCAL PRESS ISBN 978 1 925726 61 9

Phonic & Word Knowledge

UNIT 22

AC9E4LY09, AC9E4LY11

Syllables and the schwa sound

Remember! Words with two or more syllables have one or more stressed syllables and may have one or more unstressed syllables. The vowel in an unstressed syllable usually has the schwa sound. It sounds like 'uh'. There is no special letter to represent it in written words. You will only see the letters that represent the vowel sounds: a, e, i, o, u and y.

Break these words into syllables. Circle the unstressed syllable. Write the letter or letters that represent the schwa sound.

1. orbit = ________ + ________ (_____)
2. statement = ________ + ________ (_____)
3. cricket = ________ + ________ (_____)
4. surface = ________ + ________ (_____)
5. even = ________ + ________ (_____)
6. reason = ________ + ________ (_____)
7. around = ________ + ________ (_____)
8. gravity = ______ + ______ + ______ (_____)
9. powerful = ______ + ______ + ______ (_____)
10. located = ______ + ______ + ______ (_____)

Long vowel 'a'

Say each word in the word bank. They each have the long vowel 'a' sound.

straight	eight	make	space
shape	change	locate	way
	train	main	

Choose words from the word bank to complete these sentences.

11. Gravity pulls everything towards the centre of Earth in a ______________ line.
12. You can ______________ the direction of a ball by using a force.
13. Gravity stops us from floating off into ______________.
14. The ______________ of Earth is a sphere.
15. Earth is one of ______________ planets in our solar system.

The 'r' controlled vowel sound 'or'

Say each word in the word bank. They each have the vowel sound 'or'.

force	forth	ball	fall	toward
because	floor	more	orbit	core

Choose words from the word bank to complete these sentences.

16. You pump your arms and legs to make you swing back and ______________.
17. Gravity helps a cricket ______________ fall into a catcher's glove.
18. You can use ______________ to change the direction an object is moving.
19. An object with ______________ mass has more gravity.
20. The centre of Earth's mass is at its ______________.

Homophones

Write the correct homophone to complete each sentence.

21. Gravity pulls everything in a ______________ line. (straight, strait)
22. Earth is one of ______________ planets in the solar system. (eight, ate)
23. Gravity is the ______________ thing we are learning about in science. (main, mane)
24. Our team came ______________ in the cricket competition. (forth, fourth)
25. When we throw a ______________, it always lands on the ground. (ball, bawl)
26. People ______________ more on Earth than they do on the moon. (weigh, way)

Score 2 points for each correct answer! SCORE /52 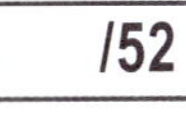 0-24  26-46  48-52

TERM 3

AC9E4LA03, AC9E4LY03, AC9E4LY04, AC9E4LY05

Imaginative text – Science Fiction

The Silver Ball of Hope (Part 3)

Other chapters of this story can be read in Units 7, 15, 31

Tor and Cassini are in the Gravalon Crater searching for the silver ball of hope. Tor looks at the dark openings of caves in the rocky walls.

"One of these must be Vulcha's lair," he calls to Cassini. His voice echoes loudly off the crater walls.

"Sh-sh!" says Cassini.

"The king says the silver ball is on a ledge near a cave," whispers Tor.

"I'll look this way and meet you around the other side," Cassini whispers back.

Tor and Cassini carefully scan the walls in the soft, blue Mylos light. Tor sees a cave high in the crater wall. There is a rocky ledge below it. "Could that be it?" he wonders. He feels a warm breath against his cheek. Thinking it is Cassini, he points to the cave. "Look Cassi," he whispers, "up there!"

Another hot breath brushes his cheek. He turns around and is staring into the huge red eyes of an enormous dragon. A roar fills the air as fire gushes from the dragon's mouth. Tor stumbles backwards.

The dragon pins Tor to the crater floor with one clawed foot. Cassini rushes to help, but the dragon whips its long tail around her.

Tor and Cassini are trapped, and they can't reach their weapons. The dragon raises its head and roars.

Source: Image from and text adapted from *The Silver Ball of Hope*, the second book in the Star Quest series by Del Merrick, Blake Education.

TERM 3

TARGETING ENGLISH HOMEWORK YEAR 4 © PASCAL PRESS ISBN 978 1 925726 61 9

Reading & Comprehension

Use these clues to complete the crossword.

Across

1. The villain of the story is ___________.
3. The king said the ball was on a ___________.
6. ___________ felt the heat on his cheek.
7. They searched in the ___________ crater.
8. They were on the planet ___________.
9. They could not reach a ___________ to use.
10. The ___________ had them trapped.
12. The dragon had ___________ on its feet.
14. They were looking for the ___________ ball of hope.

Down

2. Vulcha's ___________ was in one of the caves.
4. The dragon was ___________.
5. Tor was searching with ___________.
11. The dragon's eyes were ___________.
12. Tor pointed to a ___________ up high.
13. The cave was in the ___________ of the crater.

1		2					3				4	
					5					6		
	7											
	8						9					
10	11						12			13		
			14									

TERM 3

What I'm reading

Title: ______________________________

It's: ☐ a paper book/magazine/comic
☐ an audiobook
☐ online

It's: ☐ imaginative ☐ informative

Rating ☆ ☆ ☆ ☆ ☆

Score 2 points for each correct answer!

SCORE /30   

Grammar & Punctuation

AC9E4LA04, AC9E4LA07, AC9E4LA12, AC9E4LY06

TERM 3

Direct speech – Speech marks, commas, capital letters

Remember! Writers use speech marks, also called quotation marks ("...") at the beginning and end of what characters say. The first spoken word always has a capital letter. A comma marks off the spoken words from the rest of the sentence unless a question mark (?) or exclamation mark (!) is used.

Saying verbs show which people are talking and how they say things.

Add the missing capital letters, speech marks and other punctuation where necessary. Circle the saying verbs.

1. one of these must be Vulcha's lair Tor calls
2. sh-sh says Cassini
3. the king says it's on a ledge whispers Tor
4. I'll meet you around the other side suggests Cassini
5. oh no grumbles Tor we're trapped

Pronouns

Remember! Pronouns take the place of nouns. We use pronouns so we don't have to repeat the same nouns over again.

Read these sentences. Circle the pronouns. Write the nouns they refer to.

6. They are searching for the silver ball of hope. ______________
7. "One of these must be Vulcha's lair," he calls. ______________
8. "He says it is on a ledge near a cave," whispers Tor. ______________
9. "I'll meet you around the other side," she says. ______________
10. It pins Tor to the crater floor. ______________

Determiners

Remember! A determiner is part of a noun group. Its job is to point out (determine) which noun is being referred to. Determiners include possessive pronouns.

Examples: his, her, my, our, your, its, their, whose; as well as: the, a, an, this, that, these, those, some, most, every, each, any, what, which, one, two, three

Write appropriate determiners to complete these sentences.

11. Tor and Cassini are in __________ Gravalon Crater.
12. When Tor called to Cassini, __________ voice echoed off the wall.
13. The king sent Tor and Cassini on __________ mission to __________ planet Mylos.
14. Tor pointed to __________ cave high on __________ crater wall.
15. Tor and Cassini could not reach __________ weapons.
16. Cassini looked over __________ shoulder at Tor.
17. The dragon raised __________ head and roared.
18. __________ dragon pinned Tor to the crater floor.

Adjectives

Write an adjective to describe each of these.

19. ______________ ball
20. ______________ dragon
21. ______________ crater
22. ______________ lair
23. ______________ voice
24. ______________ Tor
25. ______________ Cassini
26. ______________ weapons
27. ______________ king
28. ______________ Vulcha

Score 2 points for each correct answer! SCORE 

TARGETING ENGLISH HOMEWORK YEAR 4 © PASCAL PRESS ISBN 978 1 925726 61 9

AC9E4LY09, AC9E4LY10, AC9E4LY11

Apostrophes for contractions and possessives

Remember! Apostrophes are used in contractions when two words are shortened into one word.
They are also used to show possession, or ownership.

Read these sentences. Circle the words with an apostrophe. Write C for contraction. Write P for possession.

1. _____ "One of these must be Vulcha's lair," said Tor.
2. _____ "I'll look this way and meet you around the other side," Cassini whispers back.
3. _____ There's a rocky ledge high up in the crater wall.
4. _____ A roar fills the air as fire gushes from the dragon's mouth.
5. _____ Tor and Cassini can't reach their weapons.
6. _____ Tor's cheek felt hot when a hot breath brushed it.
7. _____ Tor's pleased that he found the cave where the silver ball might be.
8. _____ The dragon's tail whipped around Cassini.
9. _____ Cassini's voice was a low whisper.
10. _____ They couldn't have known about the dragon before it attacked.

Draw lines to match these contractions with their meanings.

11. they're	there is
12. doesn't	you have
13. could've	could have
14. there's	they are
15. you've	you are
16. you're	does not

Consonant trigraphs 'tch' and 'dge'

A trigraph is a group of three letters that represents one sound.
Examples: tch in watch dge in ledge
The trigraph tch spells the 'ch' sound. It is never used at the beginning of a word. It usually follows a short vowel sound.
The trigraph dge spells the 'soft g' or 'j' sound. It usually follows a short vowel sound.

Read the words. Draw lines to match them to the pictures.

17. match
18. patch

19. witch

20. badge

21. hedge
22. ledge

23. fudge
24. judge
25. bridge
26. watch

Choose words from exercises 17 – 26 to complete these sentences.

27. The king thought the ball was on a _______________ near a cave.
28. Cassini could not _______________ as Tor climbed up higher.
29. The _______________ was broken so they could not cross the river.
30. Tor and Cassini wore a _______________ on their shirts to identify them.
31. Tor and Cassini were no _______________ for the dragon without their weapons.
32. They could not _______________ how far the ledge was from the floor of the cave.

Word building

Add the letters 'ush' to complete each of these words.

33. br_______	38. cr_______
34. g_______	39. fl_______
35. r_______	40. b_______
36. p_______	41. m_______
37. bl_______	

Did you notice that two words had a different vowel sound? Write them here.

42. _______________________________
43. _______________________________

Score 2 points for each correct answer! SCORE /86

TERM 3

AC9E4LA02, AC9E4LE02, AC9E4LE03

Movie review: *Wonka*

Wonka

You can watch *Wonka* on Netflix.

Reviewed by Anna 10, Queensland.

Roald Dahl is my favourite author, and *Charlie and the Chocolate Factory* is my favourite book. I have read it millions of times. I have already watched a couple of movies about Charlie. They weren't as good as the book, so I wasn't sure if I wanted to see this one at first. When I found out it wasn't about the book (it's a prequel), I decided to give it a try.

It was wonderful. It is one of the best movies I've seen. It's all about Willy Wonka when he was young. He travels all over the world collecting chocolate recipes. Then he uses his imagination and magic to set up his chocolate shop. It's so cool.

Timothée Chalamet plays Willy. He's awesome. I think he's the perfect Willy. He is funny and kind and looks after his friends, especially Noodle. I like her too. Willy is great at defeating the villains and the policeman, who is always trying to catch him.

The songs and dance numbers are good too. There's a little bit of violence, but it's not that bad. I didn't mind because I knew Willy was going to be okay in the end. I laughed out loud more times than I cried.

I think the movie is super sweet, super magical and super delicious with all that chocolate. It is suitable for children who are over 8. Even if they have read the book, they won't be disappointed. I give it 5 plus stars. I can't wait to see it again.

TARGETING ENGLISH HOMEWORK YEAR 4 © PASCAL PRESS ISBN 978 1 925726 61 9

Review

Shade the bubble next to the correct answer. Write the answer on the line where appropriate.

1. Have you seen *Wonka*?
   - ◯ Yes
   - ◯ No
   - ◯ Unsure

2. After reading this review, would you like to see *Wonka*?
   - ◯ Yes
   - ◯ No
   - ◯ Unsure

3. Which words or phrases in the review help you decide?

   ____
   ____
   ____
   ____

4. List some movies that you have seen. Circle your favourite.

   ____
   ____
   ____
   ____

Now you can write a review of your favourite movie so that others can decide whether to watch it or not.

1. About the movie

   Title: ______________________________

   Where/How can you watch it?

   ____

2. Circle the word that best describes the type of movie.

   comedy science fiction superhero
   family adventure mystery
   scary detective action
   fantasy drama musical

   If the type of movie is not listed, write it here:

   ____

3. How is the movie presented? (Choose any that apply.)
   - ◯ animated
   - ◯ puppets
   - ◯ real people or animals
   - ◯ people acting
   - ◯ other ______________________

4. When did you see the movie?

   ____
   ____

5. Where did you watch it?

   ____
   ____

6. How many times have you seen it?

   ____
   ____

7. Who did you watch the movie with?

   ____
   ____

8. What made you choose to watch it the first time?

   ____
   ____
   ____
   ____
   ____
   ____

TERM 3

Review

The characters

⑨ What do you know about the main character; for example, their name, where they live, what they like doing, what they look like? Include anything you find interesting about the character.

⑩ What do you know about one of the other characters; for example, their name, where they live, what they like doing, what they look like? Include anything you find interesting about the character.

⑪ Who is your favourite character?

Why?

The setting

⑫ When does the movie take place?

- ◯ in the past, a long time ago
- ◯ in the past, not long ago
- ◯ in the present
- ◯ in the future
- ◯ not sure

⑬ Where does the movie take place? Is it a real location or a fictional place?

⑭ List things that can be seen, heard or smelled in the location.

Seen

Heard

Smelled

TERM 3

TARGETING ENGLISH HOMEWORK YEAR 4 © PASCAL PRESS ISBN 978 1 925726 61 9

Review

The plot

⑮ What happens in the beginning of the movie?

Complication

⑯ What problem does the character have to overcome?

⑰ How does the movie end?

⑱ What is your favourite part of the movie?

Why?

Draw your favourite part.

⑲ Who else might like to watch this movie? Who do you recommend it for?

⑳ How many stars do you give it?

Reading & Comprehension

The Importance of Rest and Relaxation

Rest and relaxation are important for growing bodies. There needs to be a balance between exercise and rest. Too much of either can harm your body. Sleeping is the best way to have a proper rest. You need to sleep to give your body a little holiday. You rest your brain and muscles and replenish your energy sources.

Get some sleep!

Children 5–12 years need 10 or 11 hours of sleep each night. When your body doesn't get enough hours of rest, you may feel tired or irritable. You may be unable to think clearly. Researchers believe too little sleep can affect growth and your immune system (which helps keep you from getting sick).

Try relaxing!

For relaxation, some electronic games or TV is fine, but limit this to less than 2 hours of 'screen time' per day. Do some fun activities with your family instead. Why not go for walks after dinner – and take the dog too? Perhaps go to the park and ride your bike. You don't need to exercise in a formal way, just try to put some fun physical activities into your day.

Source: Text adapted from *Components of an Active Lifestyle* by Rose Inserra, Blake Education.

Shade the bubble next to the correct answer. Write the answer on the line where appropriate.

1. **Which of these is important for growing bodies? (Choose any that apply.)**
   - ◯ rest
   - ◯ exercise
   - ◯ relaxation
   - ◯ electronic games

2. **What does there need to be a balance between?**
   - ◯ electronic games and TV
   - ◯ school and homework
   - ◯ exercise and rest

3. **What is the best way to have a proper rest?**
   - ◯ holiday
   - ◯ sleep
   - ◯ electronic games

4. **What happens when you rest? (Choose any that apply.)**
   - ◯ You rest your brain.
   - ◯ You rest your muscles.
   - ◯ You snore.
   - ◯ You replenish your energy sources.

5. **How much sleep do children aged 5 to 12 years need each night?**
   - ◯ 5–12 hours
   - ◯ 10–11 hours
   - ◯ all night

6. **Which of these may happen if you don't get enough sleep? (Choose any that apply.)**
   - ◯ You may feel tired.
   - ◯ You may be irritable.
   - ◯ You may be unable to think clearly.
   - ◯ You may get sick.

7. **What is the job of your immune system?**
   - ◯ It helps you sleep.
   - ◯ It helps keep you from getting sick.
   - ◯ It helps you exercise.

8. **How much screen time (electronic games and TV) should you get each day?**
   - ◯ as much as you want
   - ◯ at least 2 hours
   - ◯ less than 2 hours

9. **What are some fun activities families can do when reducing screen time? (Choose any that apply.)**
   - ◯ electronic games
   - ◯ go for a walk
   - ◯ go for a bike ride
   - ◯ go to the park

10. **What are some ways that you and your family fit fun physical activities into your day?**

____

____

Score 2 points for each correct answer! SCORE /20 0-8 10-14 16-20

TARGETING ENGLISH HOMEWORK YEAR 4 © PASCAL PRESS ISBN 978 1 925726 61 9

Grammar & Punctuation

Simple, compound and complex sentences

Circle the **verbs** or **verb groups** in these sentences. Underline the **main clause**. Write **S** for a **simple** sentence, **C** for a **compound** sentence and **X** for a **complex** sentence.

1. _____ Rest and relaxation are important for growing bodies.
2. _____ You rest your brain and muscles and replenish your energy sources.
3. _____ When your body doesn't get enough hours of rest, you may feel tired or irritable.
4. _____ For relaxation, some electronic games or TV is fine, but limit this to less than 2 hours of 'screen time' per day.
5. _____ Do some fun activities with your family instead.

Adverbial phrases and prepositions

Highlight the **verb** and underline the **adverbial phrase** in each sentence. Circle the **preposition** if there is one. Write what the adverbial phrase tells about the verb: **H** (how), **T** (time/when), **P** (place/where) or **W** (why).

6. _____ For relaxation, some electronic games or TV is fine.
7. _____ Go for walks with your family after dinner.
8. _____ Your immune system helps keep you from getting sick.
9. _____ You could ride your bike to the park.
10. _____ You should try to put some fun physical activities into your day.

Adverbial clauses

Circle the **verbs** or **verb groups** in these complex sentences. Underline the **adverbial clauses**. Write what the adverbial clause tells about the main clause: H, T, P, or W.

11. _____ When your body doesn't get enough hours of rest, you may feel tired or irritable.
12. _____ You may be unable to think clearly if you haven't had enough sleep.
13. _____ You need 10–11 hours of sleep each night so your body and mind rest.
14. _____ You shouldn't play electronic games for too long because you need physical activity too.
15. _____ Although Anna loved playing video games, she knew she should ride her bike more.

Verb tense – Adding 'ed' and 'ing'

Write the **past** and **present continuous** forms of these verbs.

	Base verb	Past tense	Present continuous
16	need		
17	balance		
18	sleep		
19	rest		
20	believe		

Proper nouns

Rewrite these **proper nouns** correctly.

21. australia ______________________
22. stayin' alive fitness centre ______________________
23. anzac day ______________________
24. on the road bicycles ______________________
25. parkside road ______________________

TERM 3

Grammar & Punctuation

Direct and indirect speech.

Rewrite these sentences with correct punctuation.

26. Turn off the TV now said Mum.
27. Can't I watch just 5 more minutes begged Anna.
28. Okay said Mum. Just 5 more minutes. Then we'll go to the park.
29. Can I ride my bike asked Anna.
30. Sure said Mum. Let's all ride our bikes.

Synonyms and antonyms

Write one **synonym** and one **antonym** for each of these words.

	Synonym	Antonym
31. rest	______	______
32. tired	______	______
33. believe	______	______
34. sick	______	______
35. little	______	______

Emotive words

Circle the **emotive words** in each of these sentences.

36. Rest and relaxation are important for growing bodies.
37. There needs to be a balance between exercise and rest.
38. Sleeping is the best way to have a proper rest.
39. You may be unable to think clearly.
40. For relaxation, some electronic games or TV is fine.

Adjectives

Circle the **adjectives** in these sentences.

41. Researchers believe too little sleep can affect growth and your immune system.
42. You may feel tired or irritable.
43. Some electronic games or TV is fine.
44. Try to put some fun physical activities into your day.

Score 2 points for each correct answer!

Phonic & Word Knowledge

Apostrophes for contractions

Write the **contraction** formed by joining these pairs of words.

1. does + not = ______
2. I + would = ______
3. can + not = ______
4. you + are = ______
5. we + had = ______
6. do + not = ______
7. have + not = ______
8. she + is = ______
9. could + have = ______
10. could + not = ______

Suffixes –ion, –tion and –ation

Draw lines to match **nouns** with the **verbs** they are built from.

11. relaxation	**a** irritate
12. action	**b** immunise
13. vacation	**c** relax
14. irritation	**d** act
15. immunisation	**e** vacate

Syllables

Break these words into **syllables**. Circle the **unstressed** syllable. Write the letter or letters that represent the **schwa** sound.

16. balance = ______ + ______ (____)
17. energy = ____ + ____ + ____ (____)
18. tired = ______ + ______ (____)
19. proper = ______ + ______ (____)
20. children = ______ + ______ (____)
21. limit = ____ + ____ + ____ (____)

TERM 3

TARGETING ENGLISH HOMEWORK YEAR 4 © PASCAL PRESS ISBN 978 1 925726 61 9

Phonic & Word Knowledge

Plurals

Write the **plural** for these words.

(22) body ______________________

(23) researcher ______________________

(24) game ______________________

(25) exercise ______________________

(26) illness ______________________

(27) activity ______________________

Silent letters 'g' and 'k'

Circle the words in which the letter 'g' or 'k' is **silent**.

(28) gnome　　go

(29) no　　know

(30) need　　knead

(31) gnat　　give

Homophones

One word in each sentences uses an incorrect **homophone**. Circle it. Write the correct word.

(32) Their are many different ways to fit physical activity into your day. ______________

(33) It is not good for your body to have two much exercise or too much rest.

____

(34) You kneed to sleep to give your body a little holiday. ______________

(35) You rest you're brain and muscles and replenish your energy sources.

____

Words with the 'sh' sound

Read this paragraph. Circle all the words in which you hear the **'sh' sound**.

(36) – (42)

People should do some exercise every day, especially if they are not usually active. It is important to not eat too many sugary foods, except on special occasions. Exercise and rest can help you feel less anxious. Exercising in the ocean can be fun but remember to wear a sun-safe shirt.

The digraph 'gh'

Circle the words with the **'hard g' sound**, underline the words with the **'f' sound** and tick (✔) the words if the **digraph is silent**.

(43) – (50)

ghost	laugh	eight	high
rough	ghoul	sleigh	cough

The sounds 's' and 'z'

Say these words. Look at the letters in bold type. Write **S** if you hear the **'s' sound** and **Z** if you hear the **'z' sound**.

(51) _____ **s**leep

(52) _____ doe**s**n't

(53) _____ le**ss**

(54) _____ phy**s**ical

(55) _____ re**s**t

(56) _____ need**s**

Long vowel 'e'

Read this paragraph. Circle where you hear the **long vowel 'e'**. (Hint: there are 12!)

(57) – (68)

Your body needs sleep to rest and replenish your energy sources. If you don't, you may not be able to think clearly. Researchers believe too little sleep can affect your growth and your immune system (which helps keep you from getting sick.)

Long vowel 'a'

Circle the words where you hear the **long vowel 'a'**. (Hint: there are 7!)

(69) – (75)

relax　weigh　balance　harm

brain　may　able　affect

can　after　have　holiday

relaxation　park　take

TERM 3

Score 2 points for each correct answer!

AC9E4LA03, AC9E4LY03, AC9E4LY04, AC9E4LY05

Imaginative text – Narrative

Stranger on the Beach

Jake looked at the sea. He hated it.

He hated the grey waves, and he hated the beach. He had been happy at his old school. Then his dad left and everything changed.

"We'll live by the sea with your grandparents," said Jake's mum. Her mouth smiled, but she looked sad.

So they had moved house. And now Jake didn't have any friends.

The wind was cold. Jake felt drops from the waves on his cheeks.

Suddenly, Jake heard a voice.

"What's wrong with you?"

Jake looked round. It was an older boy. "I'm fine," he said.

The boy smiled. "I'm glad I'm not as 'fine' as you. You going in?"

It was a strange question. There was nowhere to go 'in'.

"The sea. Are you going in – you know – for a surf?"

Jake said no. He didn't want to say he couldn't surf. He turned his back. He wanted the boy to go away.

"I can teach you – if you want to learn," said the boy.

Then Jake turned round. "Really? You'll teach me?"

"Yes!" said the boy. "Why not? I'm Sully. You can have this wetsuit," said Sully, "and I've got an old bodyboard you can have."

Source: Text and image from *Surfing Three-Sixty* by Jane West, illustration by Robin Lawrie, Blake Education.

TERM 4

TARGETING ENGLISH HOMEWORK YEAR 4 © PASCAL PRESS ISBN 978 1 925726 61 9

Reading & Comprehension

Shade the bubble next to the correct answer. Write the answer on the line where appropriate.

1. **Where does the story take place?**
   - ◯ at school
   - ◯ at the beach
   - ◯ at the grandparent's home

2. **Who is the story about?**
   - ◯ Jake
   - ◯ Sully
   - ◯ Jake's dad

3. **How does Jake feel when he looks at the sea?**
   - ◯ happy
   - ◯ sad
   - ◯ angry

4. **Why does he feel that way? (Choose any that apply.)**
   - ◯ He'd rather be at school.
   - ◯ His dad left.
   - ◯ He hates the sea.
   - ◯ They had to move house.
   - ◯ He doesn't have any friends.
   - ◯ His grandparents are mean.

5. **Do you think Jake's mum was happy with the changes?**
   - ◯ Yes
   - ◯ No
   - ◯ Unsure

   Explain: ______________________________

   ____

   ____

   ____

6. **Why did Jake say he was fine?**
   - ◯ He was having a good time at the beach.
   - ◯ He didn't want to talk to anyone.
   - ◯ He meant the day was fine.

7. **Why did Jake think there was nowhere to go in?**
   - ◯ There were no shops or game arcades anywhere close by.
   - ◯ The waves were too big to swim in.
   - ◯ He couldn't surf.

8. **Why did Jake turn his back on the boy?**
   - ◯ He wanted the boy to go away.
   - ◯ He didn't want the boy to see that he was unhappy.
   - ◯ The boy was being mean.

9. **What did the boy say that made Jake turn around?**
   - ◯ He called him a mean name.
   - ◯ He laughed at him because he couldn't surf.
   - ◯ He offered to teach Jake to surf.

10. **How do you think Jake will feel about the sea now?** ______________________________

    Explain: ______________________________

    ____

    ____

    ____

    ____

    ____

    ____

What I'm reading

Title: ______________________________

It's: ☐ a paper book/magazine/comic
☐ an audiobook
☐ online

It's: ☐ imaginative ☐ informative

Rating ☆ ☆ ☆ ☆ ☆

Score 2 points for each correct answer!

SCORE /20   

TERM 4

Grammar & Punctuation

AC9E4LA04, AC9E4LA07, AC9E4LA12, AC9E4LY06

Direct speech – Speech marks, commas, capital letters

Remember! Speech marks are used to identify the words that characters say. The first spoken word always has a capital letter. A comma marks off the spoken words from the rest of the sentence unless a question mark (?) or exclamation mark (!) is used.

Saying verbs show which people are talking and how they say things.

Add the missing capital letters, speech marks and other punctuation where necessary. Circle the saying verbs.

1. we'll live by the sea with your grandparents said Jake's mum
2. what's wrong with you said a voice
3. I can teach you – if you want to learn said the boy
4. really you'll teach me asked Jake
5. you can have this wetsuit said Sully and I've got an old bodyboard you can have too

Pronouns

Remember! Pronouns take the place of nouns, including the names of people.

Read these sentences. Circle the pronouns. Write the nouns they refer to.

6. Jake looked at the sea. He hated it. __________
7. "We'll live by the sea with your grandparents," said Jake's mum. __________
8. So they had moved house. __________
9. It was an older boy. __________
10. "You can have this wetsuit," said Sully. __________

Possessive pronouns

Possessive pronouns, such as his, her, our, your and my, show ownership. Unlike possessive nouns, they do not require apostrophes.

Read these sentences. Circle the possessive pronouns. Write the nouns they refer to.

11. Then his dad left, and everything changed. __________
12. "We'll live by the sea with your grandparents," said Jake's mum. __________
13. Her mouth smiled, but she looked sad. __________
14. "You can have my old wetsuit," said Sully. __________
15. "Will your wetsuit fit me?" asked Jake. __________

Text connectives

Remember! Text connectives are words and phrases that join ideas together throughout a text.

Examples: although, however, therefore, consequently, because, later, until, then, so, as a result, meanwhile, afterwards, on the other hand, firstly, after lunch, later that day

Reread the text. Write the text connectives you find here.

16 – 21

__________ __________

__________ __________

__________ __________

Antonyms

Remember! Antonyms are words with opposite meanings.

Write antonyms for these words from the story.

22. hated __________
23. happy __________
24. smiled __________
25. friends __________
26. older __________
27. question __________

Score 2 points for each correct answer!

SCORE /54   

0-24 26-48 50-54

TERM 4

TARGETING ENGLISH HOMEWORK YEAR 4 © PASCAL PRESS ISBN 978 1 925726 61 9

Phonic & Word Knowledge

AC9E4LY09, AC9E4LY10, AC9E4LY11

Compound words

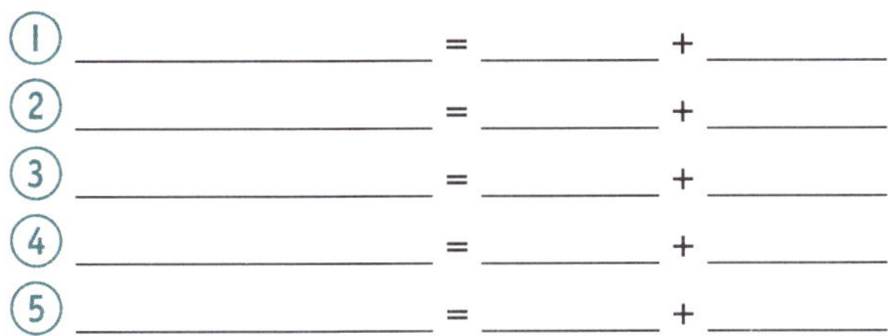

Remember! A compound word is two words joined together to make one word.

Example: no + **thing** = no**thing**

There are 5 compound words in the text. Write them here. Write the two smaller words.

① ________________ = ________ + ________

② ________________ = ________ + ________

③ ________________ = ________ + ________

④ ________________ = ________ + ________

⑤ ________________ = ________ + ________

Digraphs, trigraphs and blends

Remember! A digraph is a combination of two letters that make one sound, and a trigraph is a combination of three letters that make one sound.

A blend is when two or three letters blend while each makes their own sound.

Say these words. Look at the letters in bold. Write D (digraph), T (trigraph) or B (blend).

⑥ _____ **gr**ey

⑦ _____ **gr**andparents

⑧ _____ **fr**iends

⑨ _____ **gl**ad

⑩ _____ tea**ch**

⑪ _____ **ch**anged

⑫ _____ **sm**iled

⑬ _____ **dr**ops

⑭ _____ **str**ange

⑮ _____ wa**tch**

Homophones

Choose the correct homophone to complete these sentences.

⑯ Jake did not ______________ if he wanted to surf. (know, no)

⑰ Jake wondered ______________ the voice was coming from. (wear, where)

⑱ Sully was an older ______________ who knew how to surf. (boy, buoy)

⑲ Jake found it hard to ______________ Sully over the noise of the waves. (hear, here)

⑳ Jake was surprised when he ______________ what Sully said. (heard, herd)

Syllables

Count the number of syllables in each word, then write them in the correct box.

surf	question	waves
bodyboard	nowhere	wetsuit
grandparents	strange	suddenly

One syllable
㉑
㉒
㉓

Two syllables
㉔
㉕
㉖

Three syllables
㉗
㉘
㉙

Break these words into syllables. Circle any syllables with the schwa sound.

㉚ hated = __________ + __________

㉛ happy = __________ + __________

㉜ sudden = __________ + __________

㉝ parents = __________ + __________

㉞ around = __________ + __________

㉟ didn't = __________ + __________

Score 2 points for each correct answer! SCORE /70 0-32 34-64 66-70

AC9E4LA03, AC9E4LY03, AC9E4LY04, AC9E4LY05

Informative text – Procedure

Pumpkin Soup

Great for school lunches in an insulated container!

Ingredients

I tbsp olive oil

I onion, finely diced

I kg butternut pumpkin, diced into I–2 cm cubes

3 medium potatoes, diced into I–2 cm cubes

2 cloves garlic, crushed

I tsp finely chopped fresh rosemary

2 cups vegetable stock

2 cups water

Salt and pepper (to taste)

Utensils

Large soup pot

Spoon

Stick blender

Method

Ask an adult for help with the chopping and cooking.

1. Heat the oil and fry the onions gently in the pot over a medium heat.
2. Add the garlic, pumpkin, potato and rosemary. Fry gently for another 5 minutes, stirring frequently. Add small amounts of hot water to stop it from sticking, if necessary.
3. Add 2 cups of stock and 2 cups of water. Season with salt and pepper. Bring to the boil.
4. Turn the heat to low as soon as the soup is boiling. Simmer for about 30 minutes until the potato and pumpkin are soft and starting to fall apart.
5. Remove from the heat. Cool for about 5 minutes.
6. Blend the mixture until smooth.
7. Serve warm with soft bread rolls!

TARGETING ENGLISH HOMEWORK YEAR 4 © PASCAL PRESS ISBN 978 1 925726 61 9

Reading & Comprehension

Shade the bubble next to the correct answer.

1. What is an ingredient?
   - ◯ an item of food
   - ◯ a tool to use
   - ◯ a way to do things
2. What is a utensil?
   - ◯ an item of food
   - ◯ a tool to use
   - ◯ a way to do things
3. What is a method?
   - ◯ an item of food
   - ◯ a tool to use
   - ◯ a way to do things
4. What does **dice** mean?
   - ◯ roll a dice
   - ◯ cut into cubes
   - ◯ measure
5. Which of these ingredients do you **not** cut?
   - ◯ pumpkin
   - ◯ potato
   - ◯ rosemary
   - ◯ vegetable stock
6. What is a stick blender used for?
   - ◯ to blend sticks
   - ◯ to blend the mixture
   - ◯ to dice the potatoes
7. What do you have to do first?
   - ◯ cook the pumpkin and potato
   - ◯ fry the onions
   - ◯ heat the vegetable stock
8. What does **simmer** mean?
   - ◯ boil
   - ◯ cook on a high heat
   - ◯ cook on a low heat
9. How long do you simmer the soup?
   - ◯ 5 minutes
   - ◯ 30 minutes
   - ◯ one hour
10. How could you take some soup to school for your lunch?
    - ◯ in an insulated container
    - ◯ in a paper bag
    - ◯ in a plastic bag

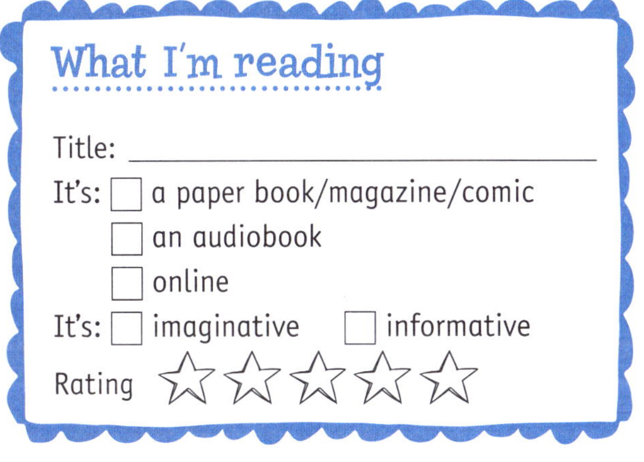

TERM 4

Score 2 points for each correct answer! SCORE /20

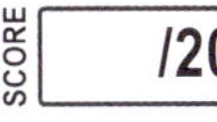

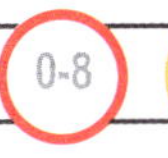

Grammar & Punctuation

AC9E4LA09, AC9E4LA11, AC9E4LA12, AC9E4LY06

Lists

Ingredients are the food items required for a recipe. They are usually written as a list with the items listed in the order that they are required, as in the pumpkin soup recipe.

Read the steps in this recipe. Write a list of the ingredients required.

Put the oats, bananas, eggs, seeds, dates, baking powder and 50 ml of the milk into a blender. Blitz to make a batter. Blitz in enough extra milk to make the batter pourable, then pour into the cases and top with your choice of either blueberries, a raspberry, a couple of date slices or a sprinkling of chopped nuts. Bake for 15–20 mins until well risen and lightly golden.

1. ______
2. ______
3. ______
4. ______
5. ______
6. ______
7. ______
8. ______

Utensils are the tools required for preparing a recipe. They are also written as a list.

In the pumpkin recipe, only the utensils needed for the actual cooking are listed. Other utensils would be required for preparing the vegetables and serving the soup. Write a list of the other utensils required.

9. ______
10. ______
11. ______
12. ______
13. ______
14. ______
15. ______

Commands – Doing verbs

Remember! Each step in the method of a recipe is a command. It tells you what to do. It begins with a doing verb. Some steps have two or more commands as they are related.

List the doing words you find in each step of the method for making pumpkin soup. (Hint: there may be more than one in each step.)

16. ______
17. ______
18. ______
19. ______
20. ______
21. ______
22. ______
23. ______
24. ______
25. ______
26. ______
27. ______

Past tense verbs

Rewrite these commands in the past tense as if you have already done them.

28. Heat the oil and fry the onions gently.
______
______

29. Add 2 cups of stock and 2 cups of water.
______
______

30. Turn the heat to low as soon as the soup is boiling.
______
______

31. Serve warm with soft bread rolls!
______
______

Score 2 points for each correct answer!

SCORE /62   0-28  30-56  58-62

TARGETING ENGLISH HOMEWORK YEAR 4 © PASCAL PRESS ISBN 978 1 925726 61 9

Phonic & Word Knowledge

AC9E4LY09, AC9E4LY10, AC9E4LY11

Words ending with -ture

Words that end with '-ture' are usually nouns. Because the syllable is often unstressed, it is pronounced 'chuh' with the schwa sound.

Example: mix**ture** (a substance formed by mixing two or more other substances)

Exceptions: ma**ture** and minia**ture** (both are pronounced 'choor' like **poor** and **your**.)

Say each word in the word bank. They each end with the syllable 'ture'.

mixture	nature	future	creature
capture	pasture	fracture	culture
adventure	fixture	gesture	lecture
picture	nurture	texture	vulture
	moisture	puncture	

Choose words from the word bank to complete these sentences.

1. The soup is a ______________ of pumpkin, potato and other flavours.
2. The artist painted a still life ______________ of pumpkin soup.
3. The pumpkin soup was quite lumpy in ______________.
4. The cook got a ______________ in her tyre on her way to the store.
5. A big bowl of soup waited for them at the end of their ______________.

The letter 'o'

The letter 'o' is used to represent different vowel sounds, including the short vowel sound 'o' as in dog and the long vowel sound as in hole.

It also combines with other vowels to form digraphs.

Examples: **oa** (boat), **oi** (toil), **oy** (boy), **or** (corn), **ow** (cow), **ou** (out), **oo** (moon, book)

At the beginning of some words, it represents 'wuh'.

Examples: **o**ne, **o**nce

It can also represent the schwa sound 'uh' at the beginning of words.

Examples: **o**nion, **o**ther

Read these sentences. Circle the words that begin with the letter 'o'. Write S for the short 'o' vowel sound, L for the long 'o' vowel sound, W for the 'wuh' sound, U for the schwa sound and D for a sound represented by a digraph.

6. _____ Gently fry the onions until they are soft.
7. _____ Heat the oil in the frying pan.
8. _____ If you open the drawer, you will find the spoon.
9. _____ We often make pumpkin soup for school lunches.
10. _____ We make the pumpkin soup in one big pot.
11. _____ You must not omit to simmer the soup for 30 minutes.
12. _____ You can put the soup in the oven to keep it warm.
13. _____ You can have pumpkin soup or a toastie for lunch.
14. _____ I tried pumpkin soup once and I didn't like it.
15. _____ You need 2 cups of vegetable stock.

Suffixes

Add endings to these base verbs to show past tense and present tense.

	Base verb	Did (past tense)	Doing now (present tense)
16	chop		
17	cook		
18	heat		
19	fry		
20	remove		

Score 2 points for each correct answer! SCORE /40  0-18  20-34  36-40

TERM 4

AC9E4LA03, AC9E4LY03, AC9E4LY04, AC9E4LY05, AC9S4U03

Imaginative text – Poem

The Attraction Of Levitation

by H. G. Paine

"Oh, dear!" said little Johnny Frost,
"Sleds are such different things!
When down the hill you swiftly coast
You'd think that they had wings;

"But when uphill you slowly climb,
And have to drag your sled,
It feels so heavy that you'd think
'Twas really made of lead.

"And all because an Englishman,
Sir Isaac Newton named,
Invented gravitation, and
Became unduly famed;

"While if he had reversed his law,
So folks uphill could coast,
It seems to me he would have had
A better claim to boast.

"Then coasting would all pleasure be;
To slide up would be slick!
And dragging sleds downhill would be
An awful easy trick!"

Source: Published in Harper's Round Table, 1895 https://www.mirrorservice.org/sites/ftp.ibiblio.org/pub/docs/books/gutenberg/4/8/5/5/48556/48556-8.txt.

TERM 4

Reading & Comprehension

Write your answers on the lines provided.

1. What is the title of the poem?

2. Who wrote the poem?

3. Who or what is the poem about?

4. From whose point of view is the poem told?

5. What does the poem complain about?

6. Who does the speaker blame for the difficulty?

7. What does the speaker think would be a better **claim to boast**?

8. How does the speaker compare sleds going downhill to uphill?

9. Is the difference between downhill and uphill really the fault of Sir Isaac Newton?

10. What would you say to Jack Frost to explain why it happens that way?

TERM 4

What I'm reading

Title: ______

It's: ☐ a paper book/magazine/comic
☐ an audiobook
☐ online

It's: ☐ imaginative ☐ informative

Rating ☆☆☆☆☆

Score 2 points for each correct answer!

SCORE /20   

Grammar & Punctuation

AC9E4LA08, AC9E4LA11

Word order

Remember! Most poems are written with a particular rhythm or beat. The rhythm is created by a pattern of stressed and unstressed syllables.

Sometimes in a poem, the order of words in sentences is changed so that the pattern of stressed and unstressed syllables, or the rhythm, as well as the rhyme, can be maintained.

Example: When down the hill you swiftly coast.

Usually, we would say: When you swiftly coast down the hill. *Or* When you go down the hill fast.

Read these sentences. Rewrite them as we would normally say or write them.

1. But when uphill you slowly climb, you have to drag your sled.

____

____

2. And all because an Englishman, Sir Isaac Newton named.

____

____

3. If he had reversed his law so folks uphill could coast.

____

____

4. Then coasting would all pleasure be.

____

____

Adverbs, adverb groups and adverbial phrases

Adverbs, adverb groups and adverbial phrases tell how, where, when and why things happen.

Examples:

slowly	very slowly	down the hill
↑	↑	↑
adverb	adverb group	adverbial phrase

Circle the verbs and highlight the adverbs, adverb groups and adverbial phrases in these sentences. There may be more than one.

5. Down the hill you swiftly coast.
6. "Oh, dear!" little Johnny Frost sighed sadly.
7. Newton should reverse his law so folks could coast uphill.
8. Little Johnny Frost dragged his sled very slowly up the hill.
9. You can coast like a breeze down the hill.
10. I always think it would be fun to fly with wings.

Antonyms

Find antonyms (words that mean the opposite) in the poem for these words.

11. uphill _______________
12. light _______________
13. drag _______________
14. slowly _______________
15. same _______________
16. better _______________

Synonyms

Find synonyms (words that mean the same) in the poem for these words. Write them here.

17. fast _______________
18. believe _______________
19. pull _______________
20. truly _______________
21. called _______________
22. turned around _______________

Adjectives

Write adjectives that tell more about these nouns in the text.

23. sleds _______________
24. Newton _______________
25. coasting _______________
26. claim _______________

Write adjectives to tell what you think of little Jack Frost.

27. _______________

Score 2 points for each correct answer! SCORE /54 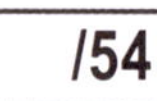 0-24  26-48  50-54 

TERM 4

TARGETING ENGLISH HOMEWORK YEAR 4 © PASCAL PRESS ISBN 978 1 925726 61 9

Phonic & Word Knowledge

UNIT 27

AC9E4LE04, AC9E4LY09, AC9E4LY11

Silent letter 'l'

In some words, the letter 'l' is not pronounced. It is silent.

Usually, when a word has the letters alm, alk, alf or alv, the 'l' is silent.

Examples: palm talk half halve

Exception: valve

In the modal verbs spelt ould, the 'l' is also silent.

Examples: could would should

There are also two words with the letters olk in which the 'l' is silent.

Examples: folk yolk

Say each word in the word bank. They each have a silent letter 'l'.

talk	walk	chalk	could
should	would	balm	calm
palm	half	calf	halves
folks	yolks	salmon	almond

Choose words from the word bank to complete these sentences.

1. Sir Isaac Newton ______________ reverse his law.
2. If Sir Isaac Newton reversed his law, some ______________ would be pleased.
3. It ______________ be good to coast uphill, if only we could.
4. It is difficult to ______________ uphill when you have to drag a sled.
5. Going downhill takes less than ______________ the time as going uphill.

Rhyming words

Write words from the poem that rhyme with these words. Write two more words that rhyme.

6. things __________ __________ __________
7. sled __________ __________ __________
8. named __________ __________ __________
9. coast __________ __________ __________
10. slick __________ __________ __________

Vowel digraph 'ea'

In some words, the vowel digraph 'ea' spells the long e vowel sound you hear in peach.

In other words, the vowel digraph 'ea' spells the short e vowel sound you hear in head.

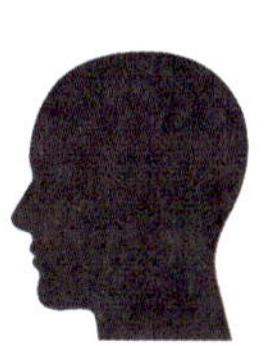

In some words, the way the digraph is pronounced depends on the context.

Examples: lead read

I put my dog on a **lead** and take him for a walk. (long e)

The sled feels like it is mad of **lead**. (short e)

I like to **read** poems. (long e)

Yesterday, I **read** the poem called 'The Attraction of Levitation' by H. G. Paine. (short e)

Say these words. Write L if you hear the long 'e' sound. Write S if you hear the short 'e' sound. Circle words that may be pronounced either way.

11. _____ heavy
12. _____ neat
13. _____ pleasure
14. _____ easy
15. _____ head
16. _____ read
17. _____ bead
18. beak
19. _____ lead
20. _____ bean
21. _____ deaf
22. _____ leap

Homophones

Circle the correct homophones in these sentences.

23 – 26 "Oh, (dear, deer)," said Little Johnny Frost. "It (seams, seems) to me that sleds should be (made, maid) of (wood, would)."

Score 2 points for each correct answer! SCORE /52   0-24  26-46  48-52

TERM 4

AC9E4LA03, AC9E4LA10, AC9E4LY03, AC9E4LY04, AC9E4LY05, AC9S4U03, AC9S4U04

Persuasive text: Advertisement

Pet Robot

ROBOBUILD

STEM
INSPIRED KIDS
Science Technology
Engineering Mathematics

REMOTE CONTROLLED

PET ROBOT

Build your own battery powered pet robot!

Best STEM Kit 2023

Everything you need, including:

- Blocks
- Wheels
- Caterpillar tracks
- Nuts and bolts
- Spanners
- Battery pack
- Easy-to-follow instructions

And much more!

EDUCATIONAL AND FUN!

Problem Solving
Creativity
Innovation

Over 400 pieces!

Impress your friends with your own remote controlled pet robot!

Build and create with the ROBOBUILD DIY Pet Robot Kit!
Suitable for beginners and experts. Durable components.
Easy-to-follow instructions with a choice of two models or design your own.

FOR AGES OVER 8

WARNING: Small parts may be a choking hazard for children under 3.

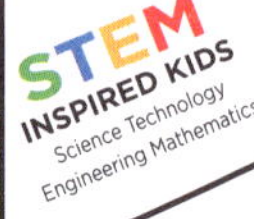

TERM 4

TARGETING ENGLISH HOMEWORK YEAR 4 © PASCAL PRESS ISBN 978 1 925726 61 9

Reading & Comprehension

Shade the bubble next to the correct answer. Write the answer on the line where appropriate.

1. **What product will be found in the box?**
   - ◯ a pet robot
   - ◯ a pet dog
   - ◯ components and instructions for building a pet robot

2. **What is the brand name of the company that made the product?**
   - ◯ Pet Robot
   - ◯ Robobuild
   - ◯ STEM

3. **What ages of children is the product suitable for?**
   - ◯ 8-year-olds
   - ◯ children under 8 years old
   - ◯ children 8 years and older

4. **Why is the product not suitable for young children?**
   - ◯ They might choke on the small pieces.
   - ◯ They would be really annoying.
   - ◯ They wouldn't be able to read the instructions.

5. **Which of these is not found on the packaging?**
   - ◯ its price
   - ◯ an image
   - ◯ what components are in the box

6. **What makes the robot move?**
   - ◯ You push it.
   - ◯ You pull it.
   - ◯ a battery

7. **How is the robot controlled?**
   - ◯ You push it.
   - ◯ with a remote control
   - ◯ by AI (artificial intelligence)

8. **Do you need to have experience building robots to build this one?**
   - ◯ Yes
   - ◯ No
   - ◯ Unsure

9. **Who do you think is most likely to buy this pet robot?**
   - ◯ children
   - ◯ teachers
   - ◯ parents
   - ◯ grandparents
   - ◯ other ____________________

   Explain: ____________________

   ____

   ____

   ____

10. **Would you like to build this pet robot?**

    ____

    ____

    Why or why not? ____________________

    ____

    ____

    ____

TERM 4

Score 2 points for each correct answer! SCORE /20    

Grammar & Punctuation

AC9E4LA12

Lists with capital letters and commas

Items in a list may be written below each other using bullet points.

On a formal list, like a menu or advertisement, they usually begin with a capital letter.

On an informal list, like a shopping list or a spelling list, they **do not** have a capital letter.

Write the items for these lists below each other. Use capital letters if needed.

1. Fun & Games: bowling, arcade games, laser tag, dodgems
2. Things to remember: toothbrush, toothpaste, pyjamas, book
3. Bring on Tuesday: guitar, music, white shirt, comb
4. Available instore: games, T-shirts, bags, merchandise

1 Have fun at FUN & GAMES!

2 Things to remember

3 Bring on Tuesday

4 ON SALE NOW!

Commas (,) are used to separate the items in a list that is written in a sentence. We do not put a comma before 'and' and the last item.

Example: I must remember my toothbrush, toothpaste, pyjamas and a book.

Add the missing commas in these sentences.

5. When you go to the beach, you need to take your togs a towel a hat and sunscreen.
6. At the resort, we could swim in the pool climb on the fort watch a movie and play tennis.
7. At school, we do English maths science art and PE.
8. I have dance lessons after school on Monday Wednesday and Friday.
9. My favourite fruits are strawberries watermelon peach plums and apples.

Complete this sentence using items from the Pet Robot package. Remember to use commas.

10. Everything you need to make a pet robot is in the box, including ______

Sentences and sentence fragments

A sentence fragment is part of a sentence. Sentence fragments are often used in advertisements and on product packaging. While they don't make sense on their own, they make sense in the context of the advertisement or packaging.

Examples: Over 400 pieces! Educational and fun!

Rewrite these sentence fragments as sentences by adding words and punctuation.

11. Build and create with ROBOBUILD.
12. Over 400 pieces!
13. Suitable for beginners and experts.
14. Best STEM Kit 2023

Score 2 points for each correct answer! SCORE /28    

TERM 4

TARGETING ENGLISH HOMEWORK YEAR 4 © PASCAL PRESS ISBN 978 1 925726 61 9

Phonic & Word Knowledge

AC9E4LY09, AC9E4LY10

Suffixes meaning 'one who'

Different suffixes are used to make nouns that mean 'one who does an action' or 'one who engages in an activity'.

Examples:

er One who teaches is a teach**er**.

ist One who does science is a scient**ist**.

ian One who does mathematics is a mathematic**ian**.

or One who creates is a creat**or**.

In some words, the noun for the person is the same as the verb for the action.

Example: One who **engineers** is an **engineer**.

Choose one of the suffixes above to change these words to nouns meaning 'one who does'.

1. One who does magic is a __________.
2. One who does art is an __________.
3. One who invents is an __________.
4. One who engages in politics is a __________.
5. One who works with electricity is an __________.
6. One who follows is a __________.
7. One who instructs is an __________.
8. One who studies physics is a __________.
9. One who works in a library is a __________.
10. One who begins an activity is a __________.

The suffix -ology

The suffix -ology means 'the study of'.

Examples:

techn**ology** ge**ology** archae**ology**

To make nouns for one who studies in these fields, we leave off the 'y' and add -ist.

Examples:

techn**ologist** ge**ologist** archae**ologist**

Write nouns for the names of people who study in these fields.

11. One who studies biology is a __________.
12. One who studies dragonology is an __________.
13. One who studies cheesology is an __________.
14. One who studies ecology is an __________.
15. One who studies climatology is a __________.

Word meanings

Draw lines to match these words to their meanings.

16. geology	**a** the study of climate
17. technology	**b** the study of dragons
18. dragonolgy	**c** the study of the earth
19. cheesology	**d** the study of equipment designed by science
20. climatology	**e** the study of cheese

Science and scientist

One who studies science is a scientist. Notice that the second 'c' in science changes to a 't' – scientist. It also changes to a 't' in scientific and scientifically.

You know the rule that 'i' comes before 'e' except after 'c'. In 'science' the 'i' comes before the 'e'. That's because the 'i' and the 'e' do not form a digraph. They are in different syllables.

Break these words into syllables. For each word, write the number of syllables, then show the syllables separated by a + sign.

21. ____ science __________
22. ____ scientist __________
23. ____ scientific __________
24. ____ scientifically __________

Score 2 points for each correct answer! SCORE /48    

TERM 4

Reading & Comprehension

AC9E4LA03, AC9E4LY03, AC9E4LY04, AC9E4LY05, AC9S4U04

Informative text – Report

The World's Longest Bridge

Designers need to use science, engineering and maths knowledge to make sure bridges stand safely. Not only do bridges have to be strong and stable in all sorts of conditions, they also have to hold an enormous amount of weight.

The Danyang-Kunshan Grand Bridge in China holds the Guinness World Record for the longest bridge in the world.

It is an elevated railway bridge between Nanjing and Shanghai and is 164.8 kilometres long. It passes over lowland rice paddies, canals, rivers and lakes. Before the bridge was built, the trip from Nanjing and Shanghai took 4.5 hours. Now, it takes only 2 hours.

The bridge took 4 years and cost the equivalent of about A$11.5 billion to build. It was finished in 2010 and opened in 2011.

About 10 000 people worked on constructing the bridge.

Made from about 450 tonnes of steel, the bridge is designed to withstand earthquakes, typhoons and other natural disasters. It is expected to last for at least 100 years.

Australia's longest railway bridge is the Sydney Harbour Bridge. It is just over 1.1 kilometres long.

Australia's longest road bridge, the Macleay Valley Bridge in New South Wales, is just over 3.2 kilometres long. It is in Fredrickton NSW. It took 10 years to make and is constructed of 941 concrete beams supported by 93 piers.

TARGETING ENGLISH HOMEWORK YEAR 4 © PASCAL PRESS ISBN 978 1 925726 61 9

Reading & Comprehension

Shade the bubble next to the correct answer. Write the answer on the line where appropriate.

1. Which bridge is considered the longest in the world?
   - ◯ Danyang-Kunshan Grand Bridge
   - ◯ Macleay Valley Bridge
   - ◯ Sydney Harbour Bridge

2. Who says it is the longest bridge in the world?
   - ◯ the article's author
   - ◯ the Guiness World Records
   - ◯ everybody

3. How long is the bridge?
   - ◯ 164.8 kilometres
   - ◯ 4.5 kilometres
   - ◯ 3.2 kilometres

4. What is the bridge made from?
   - ◯ steel
   - ◯ concrete
   - ◯ timber

5. What type of bridge is it?
   - ◯ road bridge
   - ◯ railway bridge
   - ◯ one-way bridge

6. Which of these should **not** destroy the Danyang-Kunshan Grand Bridge? (Choose any that apply.)
   - ◯ earthquakes
   - ◯ floods
   - ◯ typhoons

7. Which of these is Australia's longest **railway** bridge?
   - ◯ Danyang-Kunshan Grand Bridge
   - ◯ Macleay Valley Bridge
   - ◯ Sydney Harbour Bridge

8. Which of these is Australia's longest **road** bridge?
   - ◯ Danyang-Kunshan Grand Bridge
   - ◯ Macleay Valley Bridge
   - ◯ Sydney Harbour Bridge

9. How much longer is the world's longest bridge than Australia's longest bridge?
   - ◯ about 100 kilometres
   - ◯ just over 160 kilometres
   - ◯ almost 450 kilometres

10. What is the closest bridge to you?

    About how long is it? ______________________

    ____

    What does it cross? ______________________

    ____

    What is it made of? ______________________

    ____

    What type of bridge is it? ______________________

    ____

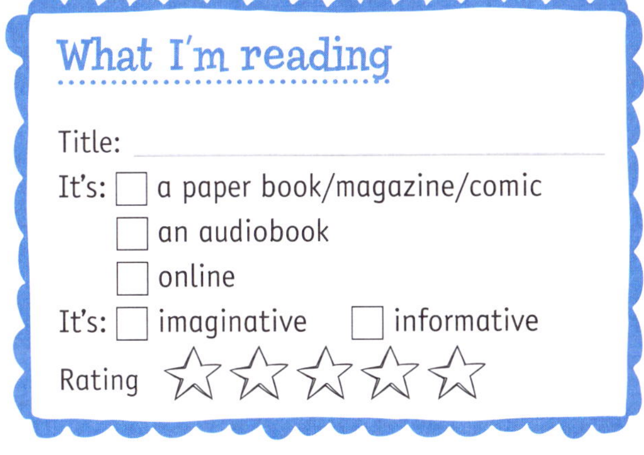

TERM 4

Score 2 points for each correct answer!

SCORE /20

Grammar & Punctuation

AC9E4LA04, AC9E4LA06

Sentences – Simple, compound and complex

Remember! A simple sentence is made up of one independent clause.

A compound sentence is made up of two or more independent clauses joined by conjunctions.

A complex sentence is made of one main (or independent) clause and one or more dependent clauses. They may be joined by conjunctions or relative pronouns.

Remember! In some sentences, the subject may be 'understood'.

Read these sentences. Circle the verbs. Write S for a simple sentence, C for a compound sentence and X for a complex sentence.

1. _____ The Danyang-Kunshan Grand Bridge in China holds the Guinness World Record for the longest bridge in the world.
2. _____ It is an elevated railway bridge between Nanjing and Shanghai and is 164.8 kilometres long.
3. _____ The bridge, which took 4 years to complete, cost the equivalent of about A$11.5 billion to build.
4. _____ About 10 000 people worked on constructing the bridge.
5. _____ Before the bridge was built, the trip from Nanjing and Shanghai took 4.5 hours.

Dependent clauses – Adverbial and adjectival clauses

Remember! An adverbial clause gives more information about the verb in the principal clause. It tells us how, when, where, why or for how long things are done or are happening.

Example: Before the bridge was built, the trip from Nanjing and Shanghai took 4.5 hours.

When did the trip take 4.5 hours? Before the bridge was built.

An adjectival clause tells us more about nouns. Adjectival clauses always follow the nouns they describe.

Example: The bridge, which took 4 years to complete, cost the equivalent of about A$11.5 billion to build.

Which bridge? The one that took 4 years to complete.

Read these sentences. Underline the verbs. Highlight the dependent clauses. Circle the conjunction or relative pronoun which links the clauses. Write V for adverbial clause, write J for adjectival clause.

6. _____ The Danyang-Kunshan Grand Bridge, which is in China, is the longest bridge in the world.
7. _____ It is an elevated railway bridge that runs between Nanjing and Shanghai.
8. _____ The Sydney Harbour Bridge was built before the Danyang-Kunshan Grand Bridge was built.
9. _____ While it was being constructed, about 10 000 people worked on the bridge.
10. _____ The bridge should last for more than100 years unless something unexpected happens.

Text connectives

Remember! Text connectives are words and phrases that join ideas together throughout a text. They help to sequence or place events in order.

Circle the text connectives used in this paragraph.

11 – 15

The Danyang-Kunshan Grand Bridge was completed in 2010. Before it was constructed, the journey between Nanjing and Shanghai took 4.5 hours. Now it takes only 2 hours. During its construction, about 10 000 people worked on the bridge. It will withstand most natural disasters and last for more than 100 years.

Score 2 points for each correct answer! SCORE /30 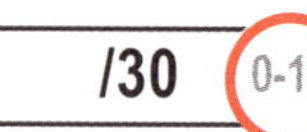  

TERM 4

TARGETING ENGLISH HOMEWORK YEAR 4 © PASCAL PRESS ISBN 978 1 925726 61 9

Phonic & Word Knowledge

AC9E4LY09

Suffixes

Suffixes are added to base verbs to change the tense.

Examples: -ed, -ing

They are also added to change verbs into nouns.

Examples: -ion, -ation, -ment, -er, -ist

However, some nouns are the same as the base verb.

Example: design

Some nouns are the same as a form of the verb.

Example: building

Complete this table to show words built from the **base verbs**.

	Base verb	Past tense	Present contin-uous	Noun	'One who' noun
1	construct				
2	elevate				
3	build				
4	design				
5	expect				
6	support				

Choose a word from the completed table to complete these sentences.

7. Over 10 000 people worked on the ________________ of the Danyang-Kunshan Grand bridge.
8. They are ________________ the Danyang-Kunshan Grand Bridge to stand for 100 years.
9. Everyone ________________ construction of the much-needed bridge.
10. The Sydney Harbour Bridge is the longest railway bridge ________________ in Australia.
11. The ________________ included concrete beams in the plan.
12. The designers said they would ________________ the bridge over lowlands, canals, rivers and lakes.

The prefix 'with'

Write **with** at the beginning of each word. Then draw lines to match the words to their meaning.

13. ________stand
14. ________out
15. ________hold
16. ________in
17. ________draw

a hold something back
b resist, stand up against
c inside
d remove or take away
e in the absence of

Syllables

Break these words into **syllables**. For each word, write the number of syllables, then show the syllables separated by a + sign. Circle any syllables with the **schwa** sound.

18. _____ designers ________________
19. _____ engineering ________________
20. _____ conditions ________________
21. _____ amount ________________
22. _____ railway ________________
23. _____ construction ________________
24. _____ kilometres ________________
25. _____ longest ________________

Compound words

Find **compound words** in the text that begin with each of these words.

26. rail ________________
27. low ________________
28. with ________________
29. earth ________________

Score 2 points for each correct answer!

TERM 4

Informative text – Checklist

Play it Safe - Checklist

The first time you try anything like playing a new sport, or even playing at home or in the playground, safety checks are important. The better prepared you are, and the better you know the safety concerns, rules or laws, the safer you will be.

Check this safety checklist before you start any activity. (Not all these points apply everywhere.)

- Where is it safe to play? (e.g. safe play zones like an oval or fenced area, or within the barriers or flags)
- What are the danger zones? (e.g. traffic areas, car park, in the midday sun, pedestrians, blind spots, steep slopes, rough terrain)
- Am I wearing the right protection? (e.g. hat, boots, pads, sunscreen and goggles)
- Does my equipment work? (e.g. brakes, lifejacket to fit my weight, recharged batteries)
- Do I know the rules? (e.g. trampoline must have a spotter, swim between the flags)
- Do I need adult supervision (e.g. lifeguard)
- Should I have a partner? (Never swim alone, even in a swimming pool)
- Will I need a water bottle? Food?
- Have I read the map and compass accurately? Do I know distances or how long the activity will take?

Source: Text from *Passport to Safety* by Hazel Edwards and Goldie Alexander, Blake Education.

TARGETING ENGLISH HOMEWORK YEAR 4 © PASCAL PRESS ISBN 978 1 925726 61 9

Reading & Comprehension

Shade the bubble next to the correct answer. Write the answer on the line where appropriate.

1. When are safety checks important?
   - ◯ when you try something new
   - ◯ every time you do something
   - ◯ every day

2. Why are safety checks important? (Choose any that apply.)
   - ◯ to keep you busy
   - ◯ to help keep you safe
   - ◯ to give you something to do

3. Do all the safety checks apply to everything you do?
   - ◯ Yes
   - ◯ No
   - ◯ Unsure

4. What are some danger zones? (Choose any that apply.)
   - ◯ playground
   - ◯ road
   - ◯ carpark
   - ◯ steep slopes
   - ◯ pools

5. What are some forms of protection that might be worn? (Choose any that apply.)
   - ◯ hat
   - ◯ boots
   - ◯ goggles
   - ◯ flags
   - ◯ sunscreen

6. What type of safety equipment might need to be checked? (Choose any that apply.)
   - ◯ goggles
   - ◯ lifejacket
   - ◯ batteries
   - ◯ flags

7. Where would you be if you saw flags and a lifeguard?
   - ◯ on the crossing at school
   - ◯ in the shopping centre
   - ◯ at the beach

8. Which of these activities should you not do alone? (Choose any that apply.)
   - ◯ jump on a trampoline
   - ◯ swim at the beach
   - ◯ read a map

9. In which of these places or activities will you find safety rules? (Choose any that apply.)
   - ◯ school
   - ◯ trampoline
   - ◯ swimming pool
   - ◯ road

10. Name one of your favourite activities and write a checklist of its safety rules.

____

____

____

____

____

____

What I'm reading

Title: ______________________________

It's: ☐ a paper book/magazine/comic
☐ an audiobook
☐ online

It's: ☐ imaginative ☐ informative

Rating ☆☆☆☆☆

Score 2 points for each correct answer!

SCORE /20   

TERM 4

Grammar & Punctuation

AC9E4LA09, AC9E4LA12, AC9E4LY06

Sentences – Questions

Remember! Statements are sentences that provide information. Questions are sentences that ask for information. Questions begin with a capital letter and end with a question mark.

Questions may begin with adverbs, like how, when, where and why.

They may begin with pronouns, such as who, whom, what, which and whose.

Questions may also begin with verbs. When they begin with verbs, the verb and its helper are usually separated by the subject.

Example: **Am** I **wearing** the right protection?

Read these questions. Circle the first word. Write A for adverb, P for pronoun and V for verb. If it is a verb, circle the main verb too.

1. _____ Where is it safe to play?
2. _____ What are the danger zones?
3. _____ Am I wearing the right protection?
4. _____ Will I need a water bottle?
5. _____ Who is supervising the activity?

Write 5 questions you should ask to check if you are wearing the right protection. Remember, a question begins with a capital letter and ends with a question mark.

6. ______________________________
7. ______________________________
8. ______________________________
9. ______________________________
10. ______________________________

Read these sentences. Write S for statement and Q for question. Punctuate the sentences correctly.

11. _____ I will need a water bottle
12. _____ do the brakes on my bike work
13. _____ where is the safest place to play cricket
14. _____ it is dangerous to play on the road
15. _____ have I read the map accurately

Verb tense – Past, present and future

Remember! For simple past tense, we add 'ed' to most simple present or base verbs.

Examples:

I need I need**ed** I skip I skip**ped**

Other irregular verbs do not add 'ed'. The verb changes.

Examples:

I know I knew I wear I wore

For present or past continuous tense, we add 'ing' to the base verbs.

Example:

I read. I am read**ing**. I was read**ing**.

For future tense, we use 'will'.

Example: I **will** read.

Complete this table.

	Simple present	Simple past	Continuous	Future
16				will wear
17		knew		
18	try			
19			checking	
20	prepare			

Score 2 points for each correct answer! SCORE /40    

0-18 20-34 36-40

TERM 4

TARGETING ENGLISH HOMEWORK YEAR 4 © PASCAL PRESS ISBN 978 1 925726 61 9

AC9E4LY09

The 'r' controlled vowel sound 'or'

Say each word in the word bank. Each word contains the **vowel sound 'or'**. The letters that spell the 'or' sound are in bold.

or sp**or**t imp**or**tant bef**ore**
l**aw** b**a**ll s**au**ce d**oor**
th**ough**t f**our** b**oar**d
t**augh**t s**ure** w**ar**
f**or**ce s**aw** w**a**lk y**our**

Choose a word from the word bank to complete each sentence.

1. It is always ________________ to do a safety check first.
2. Do a safety check ________________ you try anything new.
3. Make ________________ that the surrounding areas are safe.
4. You can ride your skate________________ in the park.
5. He hurt himself because he ________________ the swing was safe, but he didn't check.
6. You should not chase a ________________ if it rolls onto the road.
7. Playing ________________ is a good way of keeping fit.
8. The tennis coach ________________ me how to do backhands this week.
9. I like to have tomato ________________ on my hotdog after a match.
10. We had a choice: we could go for a swim ________________ we could go to the cinema.

Opposites – Negative prefixes

Prefixes can be added to words to change their meaning to the opposite.

Examples:

happy – **un**happy appropriate – **in**appropriate
possible – **im**possible legal – **il**legal
respect – **dis**respect compose – **de**compose

Use a **prefix** from the box to write a word that means the opposite.

11. safe ________________
12. active ________________
13. important ________________
14. prepared ________________
15. concerned ________________
16. accurate ________________

Antonyms – Opposite meaning

Write **opposites** for these words.

17. first ________________
18. new ________________
19. anything ________________
20. better ________________
21. before ________________
22. start ________________
23. danger ________________
24. right ________________

Synonyms – Similar meaning

Write **synonyms** for these words from the text.

25. important ________________
26. prepared ________________
27. know ________________
28. activity ________________
29. points ________________
30. pedestrians ________________

Compound words

There are 8 **compound** words in the text. Can you find them all?

31. ________________
32. ________________
33. ________________
34. ________________
35. ________________
36. ________________
37. ________________
38. ________________

Score 2 points for each correct answer! SCORE /76 0-36 38-70 72-76

TERM 4

AC9E4LA03, AC9E4LY03, AC9E4LY04, AC9E4LY05

Imaginative text – Science Fiction

The Silver Ball of Hope (Part 4)

This story is an excerpt from The Silver Ball of Hope, Book 2 in the Star Quest series by Del Merrick. Read other chapters in the story in Units 7, 15, and 23.

Tor and Cassini are trapped by the dragon in Gravalon Crater. Escape seems impossible.

Suddenly a voice cries. "Oh, no you don't mister."

It's Cha. He's running across the crater, swinging his vine around his head. As the dragon turns towards him, Cha throws his lasso over its head and pulls hard.

The dragon roars and springs towards him, releasing Tor and Cassini. It tosses its head, sending Cha flying through the air. He lands on the dragon's neck. The dragon tries to shake him off, but he holds on tightly. He looks at the crater wall and sees a sparkle of silver.

"Tor, over there," he shouts. "There's the silver ball!"

Tor and Cassini rush to the crater wall. Cassini climbs up and reaches over the ledge.

"I have it!" she shouts, holding up the ball. "The silver ball of hope!"

The dragon swings around. Its eyes open wide, and it falls to its knees. It gently lowers Cha down beside Tor and Cassini and bows its head. Its heart is full of hope.

"Aw," says Cha and rubs the dragon's knobbly horns.

"So, Cha, we meet in the wrong place ... again!" says Cassini.

"But at just the right time," says Tor.

Cha smiles. "Can I keep him for a pet?" he asks.

Tor and Cassini shake their heads. "NO!"

"Think I'll call him Keva," says Cha.

Source: Image from and text adapted from *The Silver Ball of Hope*, the second book in the Star Quest series by Del Merrick, Blake Education.

TARGETING ENGLISH HOMEWORK YEAR 4 © PASCAL PRESS ISBN 978 1 925726 61 9

Reading & Comprehension

Use these clues to complete the crossword.

Across

1. Cha saw the __________ ball of hope.
7. Cha held on __________ to the dragon.
8. The __________ roared at Cha.
11. Cha said, "No you don't __________."
12. __________ was pleased to see Cha.
14. The dragon had knobbly __________.
15. Cha made a __________ from the vine.
16. Cha swung the __________ over his head.
17. The dragon fell to its __________.

Down

2. Escape from the dragon seemed __________.
3. Tor said Cha was in the __________ place.
4. The dragon made Cha __________ through the air.
5. Cassini reached over the __________.
6. __________ rescued Tor and Cassini.
9. Cha wanted to keep the dragon as a ______.
10. Cassini said Cha was in the ________ place.
13. Cha named his pet dragon __________.
14. They found the silver ball of __________.

			1	2				3				4
5		6										
						7						
8												
						9					10	
		11							12			
	13							14				
				15								
	16											
					17							

What I'm reading

Title: ______________________

It's: ☐ a paper book/magazine/comic
☐ an audiobook
☐ online

It's: ☐ imaginative ☐ informative

Rating ☆ ☆ ☆ ☆ ☆

Score 2 points for each correct answer!

SCORE /36

Grammar & Punctuation

AC9E4LA07, AC9E4LA11, AC9E4LA12, AC9E4LY06

Direct speech – Speech marks, commas, capital letters

Remember! Writers use speech marks, also called quotation marks ("…"), to show the actual words that characters say.

Punctuate these sentences correctly.

1. suddenly a voice cries oh, no you don't mister
2. there's the silver ball he shouts
3. we meet in the wrong place again says Cassini
4. can I keep him for a pet asks Cha
5. I'll call him Keva says Cha

Saying verbs

Saying verbs are used to show that someone is speaking.

Saying verbs are used for statements, commands and questions.

Saying verbs may also indicate the feelings or mood of the speaker.

Choose saying verbs from the box to complete these sentences.

said	cried	shouted	mumbled
asked	commanded	replied	
questioned	yelled	announced	
grumbled	moaned	muttered	
joked	enquired	insisted	
nagged	whispered		

6. "Get out of the way!" ______________ Cha.
7. "What are you doing here?" ______________ Cassini.
8. "You're in the right place this time," ______________ Tor.
9. "I'm really sorry," ______________ the dragon.
10. "Look in a cave on a ledge," ______________ the king.

Reported or indirect speech

Remember! Reported or indirect speech is reported by another person. It is *not* the actual words that were spoken and quotation marks are *not* used.

Rewrite these examples of reported speech as direct speech.

11. Cha yelled at the dragon to stop right there.

____

____

12. Cassini was surprised and asked Cha how he had got there.

____

____

13. Tor said that Cha had got there just at the right time.

____

____

14. Cha said that he was going to keep the dragon as a pet.

____

____

15. The dragon liked his new name Keva.

____

____

Write antonyms for these words.

16. impossible ______________
17. over ______________
18. towards ______________
19. there ______________
20. gently ______________
21. trap ______________
22. pull ______________
23. release ______________
24. open ______________
25. lowers ______________

Score 2 points for each correct answer!

TARGETING ENGLISH HOMEWORK YEAR 4 © PASCAL PRESS ISBN 978 1 925726 61 9

Phonic & Word Knowledge

AC9E4LY09, AC9E4LY10, AC9E4LY11

Syllables

Remember! Syllables are chunks of sounds in words. We can tell how many chunks of sounds there are in a word by clapping the beats. Each syllable has a vowel. Breaking words into syllables is easy when you remember the rules.

Double consonants: Break between the consonants.

Two or more consonants: Break between the consonants, but do not split a digraph or blend.

Vowels: Break before the consonant if the vowel sound is long. Break after the consonant if the vowel sound is short.

Each of these words has 2 **syllables**. Circle the **vowels** and show how to break the word into syllables using a + sign.

1. sparkle ______
2. dragon ______
3. mister ______
4. over ______
5. lower ______
6. silver ______
7. crater ______
8. lasso ______
9. escape ______
10. Keva ______

Prefixes and suffixes

A prefix or a suffix is usually a separate syllable.

Examples: across = a + cross; tightly = tight + ly; swinging = swing + ing

Show how to break these word into **syllables** using a + sign.

11. around ______
12. gently ______
13. flying ______
14. holding ______
15. again ______
16. knobbly ______

Words with 3 or more syllables

There are 4 words in the text that have **3 or more syllables**. Write them here.

17. ______
18. ______
19. ______
20. ______

Long and short vowel sounds

Say each one-syllable word in the word bank. Each word has a **short** or **long** vowel sound.

Tor	and	are	by	the	in	lands
seems	no	voice	cries	as	on	have

Sort the words into the table.

Short vowel	
21	25
22	26
23	27
24	

Long vowel	
28	32
29	33
30	34
31	

Plural (more than one)

Write the **plural** form of these words.

35. place ______
36. crater ______
37. vine ______
38. bush ______
39. sparkle ______
40. dragon ______
41. voice ______
42. grass ______
43. wall ______
44. ledge ______

Score 2 points for each correct answer!

TERM 4

AC9E4LA02, AC9E4LA10

App review: *Crazy Gears*

Crazy Gears

Crazy Gears is an app for use on an iPhone or iPad.

Reviewed by Liam 10, South Australia.

We have been learning about forces in physics at school. My little brother was playing an app on his iPad that had gears, chains and pulleys, so I thought I'd have a look.

The app is called Crazy Gears. It is published by Edoki Academy. It is meant for younger kids, so the first few levels were quite easy. The higher levels got a bit more challenging, and I had to think about what to do to get to the next level. Getting to the next level is fun because you have to get all the gears, rods and chains working together to pull the next level onto the screen.

Although the game is really for kids about 7 years old, I still had fun playing. It helped me think about how we might get our pulleys working better in our school engineering projects. I recommend all my classmates play it so they understand gears and pulleys better.

Although you do have to pay for Crazy Gears, there are no other in-app purchases or ads. Mum and Dad are happy about that. They say it's educational and helps my brother to solve problems. They like anything that helps us to learn about STEM.

Everyone in my family gives Crazy Gears a five star rating.

TARGETING ENGLISH HOMEWORK YEAR 4 © PASCAL PRESS ISBN 978 1 925726 61 9

Review

Shade the bubble next to the correct answer.
Write the answer on the line where appropriate.

1. Have you played *Crazy Gears*?
   - ◯ Yes
   - ◯ No
   - ◯ Unsure
2. After reading this review, would you like to play *Crazy Gears*?
   - ◯ Yes
   - ◯ No
   - ◯ Unsure
3. Which words or phrases in the review help you decide?

   ____
   ____
   ____
   ____
4. List some apps that you have played. Circle your favourite.

   ____
   ____
   ____
   ____
   ____
   ____
   ____
   ____
   ____
   ____

Now you can write a review of your favourite app so that others can decide whether to use it or not.

1. Title: ______________________________
2. What is needed to use it?

   ____
   ____
3. What age group is it suitable for?

   ____
   ____
4. Circle the word that best describes the type of app.

   social media language maths
   sports racing adventure
   puzzle drawing science
   messaging fighting camera

   If the type of app is not listed, write it here:

   ____
5. When did you first use the app?

   ____
   ____
6. Where do you use it?

   ____
   ____
7. How many times have you used it?

   ____
   ____
8. How often do you use it?

   ____
   ____
9. Why did you choose to use it the first time?

   ____
   ____
   ____
   ____
   ____
   ____
   ____
   ____

TERM 4

Review

⑩ **Do any of your friends or family use this app?**

- ◯ Yes
- ◯ No
- ◯ Unsure

Explain why they choose to use, or not use, this app, if you know.

⑪ **What is the app mainly about? What do you have to do in the app? What is the goal? What do you have to do to be successful?**

⑫ **Are there any special abilities or skills you need to use in the app? Explain.**

⑬ **What are the special features of the app? Describe anything you find interesting about the features.**

⑭ **What do you think of the graphics?**

⑮ **What do you think of the music?**

⑯ **Is this app like any other apps you have used? If so, in what way?**

TARGETING ENGLISH HOMEWORK YEAR 4 © PASCAL PRESS ISBN 978 1 925726 61 9

Review

⑰ How do you think this app could be improved?

⑱ What is your favourite part of the app?

Why?

Draw your favourite part.

⑲ Who else might like to use this app? Who do you recommend it for?

⑳ How many stars do you give it?

☆☆☆☆☆

TERM 4

Reading & Comprehension

Learning to Surf

Jake met Sully at the beach. Sully said he'd teach Jake how to surf. He gave Jake a wetsuit to wear and an old bodyboard.

Jake got into the wetsuit and Sully zipped it up. It was hard to breathe. Sully said it had to be tight to stop the water getting in.

The bodyboard was made of foam and plastic. Sully tied it to his wrist with elastic to stop it getting lost in the sea.

The waves looked enormous, but Jake didn't want to show that he was afraid. "I'm ready," he said.

"We will take it easy today," said Sully. "You have to learn which waves are the best."

The sea was cold. Jake held the bodyboard in front of him.

"Face the beach," shouted Sully over the noise of the waves. "When I say JUMP, jump into the wave and let it carry you in."

Then Sully yelled, "JUMP!" and Jake jumped.

The wave raced up the beach with Jake on top. It was brilliant.

Sully waved. "You're a surfer now!"

Source: Extract and image from *Surfing Three-Sixty* by Jane West, illustration by Robin Lawrie, Blake Education.

Shade the bubble next to the correct answer. Write the answer on the line where appropriate.

1. **What is the story about?**
   - ◯ learning to swim
   - ◯ learning to bodyboard
   - ◯ learning to surf

2. **Who was learning to surf?**
   - ◯ Jake
   - ◯ Sully
   - ◯ Sally

3. **Where does the story take place?**
   - ◯ at the pool
   - ◯ at the beach
   - ◯ at Jake's house

4. **What did Sully give Jake?**
   - ◯ a wetsuit and a bodyboard
   - ◯ a surfboard and a wetsuit
   - ◯ a surfboard and a bodyboard

5. **Why did Jake find it hard to breathe?**
   - ◯ He was afraid.
   - ◯ The wetsuit was tight.
   - ◯ He couldn't swim.

6. **Why does a wetsuit have to be tight?**
   - ◯ to make you swim faster
   - ◯ to look good
   - ◯ to stop the water getting in

7. **Why did Jake feel afraid?**
   - ◯ The sea was cold.
   - ◯ He hadn't been surfing before.
   - ◯ Sully was being mean.

8. **What did Sully tell Jake he had to learn?**
   - ◯ which waves are best
   - ◯ how to stand on the board
   - ◯ to watch out for sharks

9. **How did Jake feel after he tried surfing? (Choose any that apply.)**
   - ◯ afraid
   - ◯ proud
   - ◯ excited
   - ◯ eager to go again

10. **Name an activity you were a little anxious about trying at first.**

    ____

    How do you feel about it now?

    ____

    ____

    What happened?

    ____

    ____

Score 2 points for each correct answer!

SCORE /20 0-8 10-14 16-20

TERM 4

TARGETING ENGLISH HOMEWORK YEAR 4 © PASCAL PRESS ISBN 978 1 925726 61 9

Grammar & Punctuation

Direct and indirect speech

Punctuate these sentences correctly. Circle the saying verbs.

1. those waves look enormous said jake under his breath
2. we will take it easy today said sully
3. you have to learn which waves are best explained sully
4. jump shouted sully
5. i did it explained jake proudly

Pronouns

Read these sentences. Circle the pronouns. Write the nouns they refer to.

6. Sully said he would teach Jake how to surf. ______________
7. Jake got into the wetsuit and Sully zipped it up. ______________
8. Jake didn't want to show that he was afraid. ______________
9. They carried their boards into the waves. ______________
10. The wave raced up the beach with Jake on top. It was brilliant. ______________

Determiners

Read these sentences. Underline any noun groups. Circle the determiners, including possessive pronouns.

11. Jake met Sully at the beach.
12. Sully gave Jake an old bodyboard.
13. Sully tied it to his wrist with elastic.
14. Jake had to learn which waves were best.
15. Sully waved. "You're a surfer now!"

Antonyms

Write antonyms for these words from the story.

16. teach ______________
17. afraid ______________
18. best ______________
19. old ______________
20. easy ______________
21. in front ______________

Statements, commands and questions

Read these sentences. Write S for statement, C for command and Q for question.

22. _____ The waves looked enormous, but Jake didn't want to show that he was afraid.
23. _____ "Why does it have to be so tight?" asked Jake.
24. _____ The sea was cold and Jake held the bodyboard in front of him.
25. _____ "Jump!" yelled Sully.

Adverbs, adverb groups and adverbial phrases

Circle the verbs and highlight the adverbs, adverb groups and adverbial phrases in these sentences. There may be more than one. Write H (how), T (when), P (where) or W (why).

26 - 27 Jake met Sully at the beach for a surfing lesson. _____, _____

28 Sully zipped the wetsuit up tight. _____

29 - 30 We will take it very easy today. _____, _____

Adjectives

Circle the adjectives in these sentences. Write a synonym for each one.

31. Jake rode an enormous wave back to the shore. ______________
32. Jake didn't want to show that he was afraid. ______________
33. The sea was cold, and Jake held the bodyboard in front of him. ______________
34. Jake was a beginner surfer, but he did well. ______________
35. Jake could hardly breathe in the tight wetsuit. ______________

TERM 4

Grammar & Punctuation

Lists and commas

Add the missing **commas** to these sentences.

36. When Jake went to the beach, he had a wetsuit a bodyboard a towel and some sunscreen.
37. Jake thought the waves were enormous the sea was cold and the skies were grey.
38. Sully was kind clever a good friend and an amazing surfer.

Sentences – Simple, compound and complex

Read these sentences. Circle the **verbs**. Write **S** for a **simple** sentence, **C** for a **compound** sentence and **X** for a **complex** sentence.

39. _____ Jake got into the wetsuit and Sully zipped it up.
40. _____ The bodyboard was made of foam and plastic.
41. _____ The sea was cold, so Jake held the bodyboard in front of him.

Verb tense – Past, present and future

Complete this table.

	Simple present	Simple past	Continuous	Future
42				will learn
43		showed		
44	hold			
45			saying	
46	race			

Score 2 points for each correct answer!

SCORE /92 0-44 46-86 88-92

Phonic & Word Knowledge

Compound words

The words 'wetsuit' and 'bodyboard' are **compound** words.

Combine these words with either **suit** or **board** to make new compound words.

1. body ____________
2. snow ____________
3. play ____________
4. space ____________
5. swim ____________
6. black ____________
7. skate ____________
8. card ____________
9. track ____________
10. surf ____________

Digraph, trigraphs and blends

Say these words. Look at the letters in bold. Write **D** (digraph), **T** (trigraph) or **B** (blend).

11. ______ tea**ch**
12. ______ **br**ea**the**
13. ______ ti**gh**t
14. ______ **st**op
15. ______ l**oo**k
16. ______ co**ld**
17. ______ **a**fr**ai**d
18. ______ l**ear**n
19. ______ wa**tch**
20. ______ ju**mp**
21. ______ s**ai**d
22. ______ b**oar**d

Homophones

Choose the correct **homophone** to complete these sentences.

23. Sully gave Jake a wetsuit to ____________. (wear, where)
24. The bodyboard was ____________ of foam and plastic. (made, maid)
25. Jake looked at the enormous waves in the ____________. (sea, see)
26. Jake had to learn ____________ waves were best. (which, witch)

TERM 4

TARGETING ENGLISH HOMEWORK YEAR 4 © PASCAL PRESS ISBN 978 1 925726 61 9

Phonic & Word Knowledge

Syllables

Show how to break these words into **syllables** using the + sign. Circle syllables with a **schwa** sound.

(27) elastic ____________________
(28) plastic ____________________
(29) bodyboard ____________________
(30) enormous ____________________
(31) wetsuit ____________________
(32) surfer ____________________

Long and short vowel sounds

Say the words. Write **L** if you hear a **long 'o'** vowel sound. Write **S** if you hear a **short 'o'** vowel sound.

(33) _____ old
(34) _____ show
(35) _____ open
(36) _____ body
(37) _____ of
(38) _____ stop
(39) _____ foam
(40) _____ lost
(41) _____ over

Say these words. Write **L** if you hear the **long 'e'** sound. Write **S** if you hear the **short 'e'** sound. Circle words that may be pronounced either way.

(42) _____ beach
(43) _____ breathe
(44) _____ sea
(45) _____ teach
(46) _____ easy
(47) _____ read
(48) _____ ready
(49) _____ head
(50) _____ lead

Rhyming words

Write three words that **rhyme** with these words.

(51) old __________ __________ __________
(52) beach __________ __________ __________
(53) face __________ __________ __________

Suffixes meaning 'one who'

Add **suffixes** to change these words to **nouns** meaning 'one who does'.

(54) One who surfs is a ______________.
(55) One who swims is a ______________.
(56) One who teaches is a ______________.
(57) One who does mathematics is a ______________.
(58) One who studies biology is a ______________.
(59) One who invents things is an ______________.

Opposites

Find words in the text that are **opposites** of these words.

(60) new ____________________
(61) easy ____________________
(62) found ____________________
(63) loose ____________________
(64) allow ____________________
(65) miniscule ____________________

Add a **prefix** to these words to make the **opposite**.

(66) zip ____________________
(67) afraid ____________________
(68) active ____________________
(69) tie ____________________
(70) safe ____________________
(71) accurate ____________________

Synonyms

Find words in the text that are **synonyms** of these words.

(72) difficult ____________________
(73) gigantic ____________________
(74) scared ____________________
(75) prevent ____________________
(76) constructed ____________________
(77) attached ____________________

Plurals

Write **plurals** for these words.

(78) beach ____________________
(79) breath ____________________
(80) fish ____________________
(81) wetsuit ____________________
(82) wave ____________________
(83) bodyboard ____________________

Score 2 points for each correct answer!

SCORE /166 0-80  

TERM 4

MY READING LIST

Name: ______________________

____

	Title	Author	Rating	Date
1			☆☆☆☆☆	
2			☆☆☆☆☆	
3			☆☆☆☆☆	
4			☆☆☆☆☆	
5			☆☆☆☆☆	
6			☆☆☆☆☆	
7			☆☆☆☆☆	
8			☆☆☆☆☆	
9			☆☆☆☆☆	
10			☆☆☆☆☆	
11			☆☆☆☆☆	
12			☆☆☆☆☆	
13			☆☆☆☆☆	
14			☆☆☆☆☆	
15			☆☆☆☆☆	
16			☆☆☆☆☆	
17			☆☆☆☆☆	
18			☆☆☆☆☆	
19			☆☆☆☆☆	
20			☆☆☆☆☆	
21			☆☆☆☆☆	
22			☆☆☆☆☆	
23			☆☆☆☆☆	
24			☆☆☆☆☆	
25			☆☆☆☆☆	
26			☆☆☆☆☆	
27			☆☆☆☆☆	
28			☆☆☆☆☆	
29			☆☆☆☆☆	
30			☆☆☆☆☆	
31			☆☆☆☆☆	
32			☆☆☆☆☆	

TARGETING ENGLISH HOMEWORK YEAR 4 © PASCAL PRESS ISBN 978 1 925726 61 9

Answers

Term 1

Unit 1

Page 3 Reading & Comprehension

1 on Saturday
2 at Nathan's house
3 Nathan
4 getting rid of junk
5 take it to the tip
6 a billycart
7 It was dangerous.
8 Owen and Nick
9 give it a run
10 Answers will vary.

Page 4 Grammar & Punctuation

1 We carried out stacks of old books and jars.
2 Dad shook his head.
3 I wiped off more dust.
4 You can keep it.
5 Nick and Owen came round to my place.
6 We dumped stacks of old books and jars.
7 We dragged Dad's old billycart into the sunshine.
8 Dad shook his head.
9 Owen and Nick looked at The Zipper.
10 Dad made the billycart.
11 Answers may vary, e.g. How, When, Where, Why.
12 Answers may vary, e.g. How, When, Why.
13 Why
14 You're not taking it to the tip, are you?
15 Can we keep it?
16 Answers may vary, e.g. Does, Did, Will.
17 Did
18 Have
19 Answers may vary, e.g. Does, Did, Will.
20 Answers may vary, e.g. Do, Did, Will, Can.

Page 5 Phonics & Word Knowledge

1 red
2 Nick
3 junk
4 lot
5 stack
6 heavy
7 said
8 give
9 was
10 some
11 frame
12 home
13 tube
14 age
15 cube
16 piece
17 bike
18 fly
19 sheets
20 rose

Unit 2

Page 7 Reading & Comprehension

1 to make marshmallows fly
2 that the size of a force affects how far an object will travel
3 to cut the bottom off the yoghurt cup; to cut the end off the balloon
4 eating yoghurt; eating marshmallows
5 because it's tricky cutting the bottom out of a yoghurt container
6 blow it up
7 so you can draw a line where the marshmallows land
8 You pull back on the balloon and let it go.
9 No
10 Answers will vary.

Page 8 Grammar & Punctuation

1 Cut
2 Tie
3 Draw
4 Guess
5 Eat
6 – 10 Answers will vary.
11 S .
12 Q ?
13 E !
14 Q ?
15 C !
16 I tied a knot at the open end of the balloon.
17 I stretched the balloon over the rim of the yoghurt cup.
18 I went outside on a paved surface.
19 I marked each landing place.
20 I pulled back on the balloon and let it go.

Page 9 Phonic & Word Knowledge

1 pulled, pulling
2 aimed, aiming
3 hopped, hopping
4 chased, chasing
5 traded, trading
6 grabbed, grabbing
7 marked, marking
8 dropped, dropping
9 stretched, stretching
10 joked, joking
11 go – went
12 cut – cut
13 let – let
14 eat – ate
15 drive – drove
16 lay – laid
17 Place the marshmallow in the yoghurt cup.
18 You stretch the balloon over the bottom of the cup.
19 The mark on the ground shows where the marshmallow landed.
20 The adult cut the bottom off the yoghurt cup.
21 My marshmallow went farther than yours.
22 I am testing how to make the marshmallow fly farther.

Unit 3

Page 11 Reading & Comprehension

1 at Trev's house
2 His nose was bleeding.
3 something on his computer
4 He'd had his brain removed.
5 No
6 He saw dried blood under Hamish's nose.
7 He thought Trev might be an alien.
8 with nose-picking actions
9 Trev asked if Hamish had had his brain removed.
10 Answers will vary.

Page 12 Grammar & Punctuation

1 – 12 Hamish made a wild discovery. He found out that nosebleeds were a sign of alien abduction. He hurried to tell his friend Trev. Trev was picking his nose. Was it a coincidence? Could he be an alien. Hamish wasn't sure.
13 – 16 nosebleeds, friend, nose, alien
17 – 20 discovery, sign, abduction, coincidence
21 – 22 Hamish, Trev
23 "Hey, Trev!" I called through the glass.
24 "Have you had your brain removed?" asked Trev.
25 "I've just made an amazing discovery," said Hamish.
26 asked Trev
27 said Hamish
28 asked Trev
29 asked Hamish
30 said Trev

Page 13 Phonic & Word Knowledge

1 P, Trev's
2 P, Hamish's
3 C, You're
4 C, don't
5 P, Trev's
6 C, wasn't
7 C, he'd
8 C, I've
9 C, I'm
10 P, alien's
11 what're – what are
12 doesn't – does not
13 couldn't – could not
14 can't – cannot
15 you've – you have
16 I'd – I would
17 thought
18 through
19 though
20 though
21 through
22 through
23 book
24 through
25 do

Unit 4

Page 15 Reading & Comprehension

1 Runt
2 Craig Silvey
3 Allen and Unwin, 2022
4 9781761067846
5 A dog called Runt
6 Runt is fast and agile. He's good at herding sheep. He will only obey Annie.
7 Annie Shearer, a greedy landowner
8 Answers will vary, e.g. funny, exciting, Australian.
9 Yes, the reviewer gave the book 5 stars.
10 Answers will vary.

Answers

Page 16 Grammar & Punctuation

1 – 3 Runt, Annie Shearer, Craig Silvey
4 Answers will vary.
5 – 7 Upson Downs, Australia, London
8 Answers will vary.
9 – 11 Dog Show, Easter, CBCA Book of the Year Awards
12 Answers will vary.
13 Annie Shearer lives on a sheep farm in Upson Downs in Australia.
14 Those skills helped him avoid capture by other people.
15 A greedy landowner threatened to take over the Shearer's farm.
16 Annie entered Runt in a famous Dog Show in London.
17 – 20 Answers will vary.
21 – 23 Answers will vary, e.g. moments that warm your heart; laugh out loud; beautiful illustrations.

24	funny	29	unbelievable	34	best
25	strange	30	dreadful	35	worst
26	boring	31	scary	36	wonderful
27	exciting	32	horrible		
28	fantastic	33	great		

Page 17 Phonic & Word Knowledge

1	2	9	2	17	C	25	award
2	2	10	3	18	V	26	avoid
3	1	11	3	19	C	27	about
4	4	12	2	20	V	28	approve
5	1	13	V	21	C	29	agile
6	1	14	V	22	V	30	adult
7	4	15	V	23	V		
8	1	16	V	24	C		

Unit 5

Page 19 Reading & Comprehension

1 2023
2 to compare the tallest buildings in the world
3 the height of the buildings; the number of floors in the buildings; where the buildings are located; when the buildings were completed
4 Dubai
5 five
6 Makkah Royal Clock Tower
7 Burj Khalifa
8 Merdeka
9 the Q1 building on the Gold Coast
10 Answers will vary.

Page 20 Grammar & Punctuation

1 In 2023, the world's tallest building was in the United Arab Emirates.
2 The Q1 building on the Gold Coast has 78 floors.
3 The Merdeka is 679 metres tall.
4 Skyscrapers must be able to hold an enormous amount of weight.
5 The world's tallest building is over 500 metres taller than the tallest building in Australia.

6	taller tallest	14	stronger
7	shorter shortest	15	tallest
8	higher highest	16	shorter
9	safer safest	17	shorter
10	stronger strongest	18	taller
11	taller	19	shorter
12	bigger	20	shorter
13	higher		

Page 21 Phonic & Word Knowledge

1	designers; 3	16	Mecca; Mec +ca
2	knowledge; 2	17	Makkah; Mak + kah
3	safely; 2	18	bubble; bub + ble
4	stable; 2	19	design; de + sign
5	enormous; 3	20	Dubai; Du + bai
6	engineering; 4	21	scrapers; scra + pers
7	buildings; 2	22	metres; me + tres
8	strong; 1	23	Asia; A + sia
9	tall; 1	24	Beijing; Bei + jing
10	amount; 2	25	enormous; e + nor + mous
11	Shanghai; Shang + hai	26	engineer; en + gin + eer
12	complete; com + plete	27	united; u + ni + ted
13	Guangzhou; Guang + zhou	28	Malaysia; Mal + ay + sia
14	centre; cen + tre	29	Emirates; Em + ir + ates
15	Shenzhen; Shen + zhen	30	Australia; Aus + tra + li + a

Unit 6

Page 23 Reading & Comprehension

1 because they clear away dung
2 drag it under the ground; lay their eggs in it; eat it
3 No
4 to make more dung beetles
5 smell
6 Animal poo wouldn't get cleared away.; There would be a lot of flies.; The world would be dirty and smelly.
7 maggots
8 They clear away animal poo.; They help the plants grow.; They make the air smell cleaner.
9 3 cm
10 Answers will vary.

Page 24 Grammar & Punctuation

1 R Some people have clean jobs.
2 D Dung beetles collect dung left by cows and horses.
3 D Dung beetles work day and night.
4 D They drag it down under the ground, piece by piece.
5 R The world is a cleaner place with dung beetles in it.
6 P Animals couldn't walk anywhere.
7 T Maggots soon hatch.
8 H Plants grow better.
9 H Air smells cleaner.
10 P Dung beetles carry dung underground.
11 P Dung beetles lay their eggs in the dung.
12 H The beetles find dung with their sense of smell.
13 H Some dung beetles roll dung into balls.
14 P Maggots hatch out of eggs.
15 T Flies are a pest from morning till night.

Page 25 Phonic & Word Knowledge

1	beetles	14	step + ping
2	piece, piece	15	e + ven
3	people	16	some
4	behind	17	their
5	very	18	piece
6	bee + tle	19	for
7	bet + ter	20	way
8	peo + ple	21	through
9	be + hind	22	one
10	un + der	23	It's
11	col + lect	24	to
12	mag + gots	25	DUNG BEETLES
13	dir + ty		

ANSWERS

Answers

Unit 7

Page 27 Reading & Comprehension

1 C		2 M			3 T	A	R	4 V	O	S		5 P
A		Y			O			U				L
6 S	I	L	V	E	R			L		7 C	H	A
S		O						C				S
I		8 S	P	A	9 C	E	S	H	I	10 P		M
N					R			A		A		A
I		11 C			A					D		
	12 W	R	I	S	T			13 P	O	U	C	H
		A			E							
		S		14 G	R	A	V	A	L	O	N	
		H										

Page 28 Grammar & Punctuation

1 Cha was hiding in their spaceship.
2 Tor and Cassini have been sent to Mylos
3 Tor and Cassini will find the silver ball of hope
4 Tor and Cassini may have to fight for the silver ball.
5 The king is talking through a communicator on Tor's wrist.
6 P Tor and Cassini have been sent on a mission to Mylos.
7 N Neither Tor nor Cassini are pleased with Cha.
8 P Cassini was looking over Tor's shoulder at the king.
9 F They may have to fight for the silver ball.
10 F They will need to arm themselves.
11 Tor **is fixing** the damaged spaceship.
12 Tor and Cassini **were sent** to Mylos.
13 Cha **will stay** in the spaceship while Tor and Cassini search.
14 Tor **was talking** to King Padu on his communicator band.
15 Tor and Cassini **will find** the silver ball of hope.
16 Tor was working on the Tarvos because it was damaged.
17 Cassini looks over Tor's shoulder as they listen to the king's message.
18 The silver ball of hope was hidden, and it was well guarded.
19 Cassini looked at the dagger that Tor gave to her.
20 Cha was sleeping because he was tired.

Page 29 Phonic & Word Knowledge

1 S sign
2 NG sing
3 H Gravalon
4 H guard
5 NG during
6 J damage
7 S gnat
8 J gem
9 NG landing
10 H dagger
11 exit – the way out
12 extend – to stretch out
13 exceed – to go beyond expectations
14 exclude – to shut out
15 extract – to take out or remove
16 excerpt – a passage taken from a book
17 emit – to send out, e.g. light
18 eject – to throw out
19 emigrate – to move out of a country
20 exhale – to breathe out
21 – 25 quest, waist, hope, crash, sleep
26 – 30 silver, mission, planet, spaceship, brother
31 – 35 Gravalon, Cassini, pulsators, yesterday, communicator

Unit 8

Pages 30–33 Book review

Answers will vary.

Term 1 Review

Page 34 Reading & Comprehension

1 He was nervous.
2 Nick and Owen
3 on their skateboards
4 to go slower
5 with a rope tied to the front axle
6 No
7 Answers will vary; e.g. It was difficult to steer.
8 He couldn't steer it. It had no brakes. He didn't know how to stop it.
9 Answers will vary; e.g. They knew it was dangerous to go downhill too fast.
10 Answers will vary.

Page 35–36 Grammar & Punctuation

1 E Help! The billycart is out of control!
2 Q How can you make a marshmallow fly?
3 Q Did you know that nosebleeds are a sign of alien abduction?
4 E This is the best book I've ever read!
5 C Cut the bottom out of the yoghurt cup.
6 S The Burj Khalifa is the tallest building in the world.
7 C Place the marshmallow inside the yoghurt cup.
8 S Dung beetles make the world a cleaner place.
9 Q Who wrote The Golden Llama?
10 E Stop, thief!
11 Tor and Cassini repaired the damaged spaceship.
12 Nathan rode The Zipper down Birdy Street.
13 Lara shot a marshmallow out of a popper.
14 Dung beetles clean up animal poo.
15 Aliens abducted Hamish.
16 I lined up the ball, rock and feather at the edge of the table.
17 I used the ruler to push the objects off the table at the same time.
18 I watched what object hit the floor first.
19 I recorded the order in which the objects hit the floor.
20 I repeated the experiment to be sure of my results.
21 – 25 beetle, spaceship, marshmallow, building, billycart
26 – 30 worry, fear, idea, communication, hope
31 – 35 Nathan, Runt, Burj Khalifa, Mylos, Australia
36 "You're not taking it to the tip, are you?" said Nathan.
37 "So, what are you up to, Hamish?" asked Trev.
38 "Lak-tor, your mission is to find the silver ball of hope," commanded King Padu.
39 "The Burj Khalifa is the world's tallest building," Noah boasted.
40 "I think I've been abducted by aliens," whimpered Hamish.
41 – 45 Answers will vary; e.g. an enormous spaceship.
46 faster, faster
47 younger
48 tallest
49 cleaner
50 best
51 P Annie Shearer lives on a sheep farm.
52 T Nathan helped his father sort junk on Saturday.
53 P Place the marshmallow in the cup.
54 H Cut the paper with care.
55 P Run away from the aliens very fast.

ANSWERS

Answers

Page 36–37 Phonic & Word Knowledge

1 – 3 Dad, drag, stack
4 – 6 help, heavy, said
7 – 9 give, zip, nick
10 – 12 was, off, lot
13 – 15 junk, some, stuff
16 – 18 frame, paint, day
19 – 21 peace, keep, piece
22 – 24 ride, pie, fly
25 – 27 home, rope, road
28 – 30 cube, huge, new
31 knotted, knotting
32 crossed, crossing
33 told, telling
34 drove, driving
35 wrote, writing
36 rode, riding
37 fell, falling
38 shopped, shopping
39 jumped, jumping
40 flew, flying
41 you're
42 don't
43 wan't
44 I've
45 shouldn't
46 I'd
47 couldn't
48 can't
49 we're
50 didn't
51 – 54 brakes, heart, farm, soon
55 – 58 zipper, helmet, downhill, skateboard
59 – 62 billycart, marshmallow, Saturday, zigzagging
63 zip + per
64 zig + zag
65 hel + met
66 ex + hale
67 e + mit
68 a + void
69 be + fore
70 re + view
71 through
72 won
73 some
74 where
75 their

Term 2

Unit 9

Page 39 Reading & Comprehension

1 a child at school
2 on the weekend
3 in Mount Isa
4 rode a horse
5 fifty-two seconds
6 No
7 purple
8 10 years old
9 No. He had never ridden in front of so many people before.
10 excited. Answers will vary.

Page 40 Grammar & Punctuation

1 I rode a **horse** in the rodeo.
2 The runner-up got a purple **ribbon**.
3 Dad took a **video** on his phone.
4 The people clapped their **hands**.
5 I wore my cowboy **hat** in the ring.
6 have
7 has
8 take
9 takes
10 travel, travels
11 The buck was pretty wild, **but** I managed to stay on for fifty-two seconds.
12 I was good for my age range, **so** I got this purple runner-up ribbon.
13 Dad was pretty stoked **because** he used to ride broncos.
14 Dad said I did well, **but** Mum wasn't too pleased.
15 I felt pretty cool, **and** I definitely want to be a cowboy.
16 but
17 so

Page 41 Phonic & Word Knowledge

1 bronco
2 Joe
3 though
4 show
5 dough
6 rodeo – a horse-riding contest
7 radio – a device for listening to news and music sent over radio waves
8 video – a recording of moving visual images, often including sound
9 stereo – sound that comes through two or more speakers
10 audio – sound that people can hear
11 – 14 phone, horse, range, buck
15 – 18 weekend, purple, bronco, people
19 – 22 video, embarrassed, rodeo, cheerfully
23 vid + e + o
24 em + bar + rassed
25 cheer + ful + ly
26 ro + de + o
27 id
28 t
29 d
30 t
31 id
32 d

Unit 10

Page 43 Reading & Comprehension

1 There is no water in the river.
2 in Alice Springs
3 August
4 twice
5 The river was flooded.
6 They have no bottoms.
7 metal frames, bathtubs
8 People stand inside the boats and carry them.
9 pirates and Vikings
10 Answers may vary, e.g. There is no other race like it in the world. Answers may vary.

Page 44 Grammar & Punctuation

1 S A boat race without water is held in Alice Springs every year.
2 S It is the only dry river race in the world.
3 C They stand inside their boats, **and** they carry them along.
4 C In 1993 the river flooded, **so** the race was cancelled.
5 S They may be old washtubs or bathtubs.
6 The race is held in Alice Springs, and it is held on the third Saturday in August.
7 People come from all over Australia because it is the only dry river race in the world.
8 The boats are bottomless, so people carry them along.
9 Some people dress up like pirates, and some people dress up like Vikings.
10 The river flooded, so the race was cancelled.
11 P The race is held on the dry sandy riverbed.
12 T It has been running for more than 60 years.
13 P People come from all over the world.
14 W They come to watch the race.
15 H They dress up like pirates.

Page 45 Phonic & Word Knowledge

1 – 4 looked, raced, walked, dressed
5 – 8 called, covered, carried, cancelled
9 – 12 demanded, flooded, painted, waited
13 hear – heard
14 hold – held
15 run – ran
16 come – came
17 make – made
18 stand – stood
19 – 21 cancel, canoe, sandy
22 – 24 race, crazy, may
25 – 27 bath, cartoons, can't
28 – 30 call, water, all
31 – 33 yacht, washtub, was
34 – 36 pirates, about, central
37 short o
38 long a
39 schwa
40 riv + er (er)
41 Au + gust (u)
42 cen + tral (a)
43 e + ven (e)

Unit 11

Page 47 Reading & Comprehension

1 A Naughty Little Comet
2 Ella Wheeler Wilcox
3 a naughty little comet who wouldn't do as she was told
4 near the Milky Way
5 Answers will vary e.g. She would wander away. She wouldn't do what she was told. She would make fun of others.
6 The sun was the villain. He was called an ogre and he ate up the comet.
7 comet, Milky Way, stars, Sun, Mars, planets, Earth, moon

ANSWERS

TARGETING ENGLISH HOMEWORK YEAR 4 © PASCAL PRESS ISBN 978 1 925726 61 9

8 Answers may vary, e.g. She knows what will happen to the comet.
9 It vanished into the Sun.
10 Answers may vary, e.g. Do what you are told. Don't go off too far on your own.

Page 48 Grammar & Punctuation

1 Answers may vary, e.g. His favourite thing to do was eating comets.
2 Answers may vary, e.g. She was showing off in front of the Sun.
3 Answers may vary, e.g. She has disappeared from sight.
4 She, mother
5 her, comet
6 She, comet
7 who, quiet stars
8 he, Sun
9 them, they, stars
10 you, everybody
11 – 13 Anwers may vary, e.g. She loved to wander out at night and jump about and play.
The mother of the comet was a very good old star. Sun loved on stars to sup. Instead of growing cautious and of showing proper fear.

Page 49 Phonic & Word Knowledge

1	way, play (stay)	22	stir
2	star, far (bar)	23	stair
3	sup, up (cup)	24	star
4	fear, near (clear)	25	reckless – careless irresponsible
5	see, bee (flea)	26	venture – go, embark
6	mirth, Earth (girth)	27	cautious – careful, wary
7	days, praise (stays)	28	saucy – cheeky, sassy
8	trail, pail (fail)	29	mirth – fun, amusement
9	more, before (roar)	30	wan – pale, weak
10	sight, night (fright)	31	gay – happy, joyful (old fashioned/dated meaning)
11	Sun	32	mope – sulk, be sad
12	son	33	sh
13	preys	34	sh
14	praise	35	ti
15	night	36	sh
16	knight	37	s
17	sight	38	sh
18	site	39	sh
19	stare	40	sh
20	start		
21	steer		

Unit 12

Page 51 Reading & Comprehension

1 that more people should eat insects
2 Eating insects is good for people and good for the planet.
3 in hot countries
4 2,000
5 beetles, butterflies, wasps, bees, crickets
6 whole, ground into flour, in snacks
7 They are nutritious. Insects produce less greenhouse gas than cattle and sheep do. It would reduce the effects of climate change. Food would be more sustainable.
8 milk, ice-cream, snacks, beer
9 Answers will vary.
10 Answers will vary.

Page 52 Grammar & Punctuation

1	will	8	must	15	understand
2	would	9	will	16	believes
3	will	10	would	17	guess
4	can	11	think	18	notice
5	may	12	suggest	19	imagine
6	would	13	wonder	20	realise
7	should	14	know		

21 scientist – a person who studies science
22 species – a group of living things that share characteristics
23 suitable – right or appropriate
24 protein – an essential building block for life
25 nutrients – substances that provide nourishment
26 greenhouse gas – gases that trap heat in the atmosphere
27 livestock – farm animals

Page 53 Phonic & Word Knowledge

1	S	11	scent	21	yuhn
2	SK	12	cent	22	yuhn
3	SK	13	sent	23	yuhn
4	S	14	butterfly	24	shun
5	SK	15	greenhouse	25	shun
6	SK	16	however	26	shun
7	S	17	maybe	27	yuhn
8	SK	18	grasshopper	28	shun
9	S	19	livestock	29	shun
10	S	20	someone	30	yuhn

Unit 13

Page 55 Reading & Comprehension

1	in the Pacific Ocean	6	Maori, English, Pukapukan
2	the Southern Hemisphere	7	Polynesia
3	15	8	by boat
4	Rarotonga	9	1965
5	Avarua	10	after Captain James Cook

Page 56 Grammar & Punctuation

1 Most people live on the southern islands.
2 The three main languages are Maori, English and Pukapukan.
3 The capital city is Avarua.
4 The Cook Islands became an independent nation in 1965.
5 The Cook Islands is a group of 15 small islands.
6 first, people
7 small, islands
8 main, languages
9 independent, nation
10 Pacific, islands
11 The Cook Islands is a group of 15 islands in the South Pacific Ocean.
12 The capital city Avarua is on the main island of Rarotonga.
13 The three main languages are Maori, English and Pukapukan.
14 The islands were named after Captain James Cook.
15 New Zealand was in charge of the Cook Islands from 1888 until 1965.

Page 57 Phonic & Word Knowledge

1	2 Zea + land	14	divided, dividing
2	2 Fi + ji	15	made, making
3	2 low + er	16	spoke, speaking
4	3 cap + i + tal	17	controlled, controlling
5	2 En + glish	18	passed, passing
6	2 con + trol	19	explored, exploring
7	4 Rar + a + ton + ga	20	became, becoming
8	4 Puk + a + puk + an	21 – 23	passed, looked, faced
9	3 Pa + cif + ic	24 – 26	named, settled, controlled
10	4 in + de + pen + dent	27 – 29	migrated, divided, located
11	settled, settling		
12	migrated, migrating		
13	lived, living		

ANSWERS

Answers

Unit 14

Page 59 Reading & Comprehension

1. during summer
2. very hot for five or more days.
3. strong winds
4. high humidity
5. They get too hot. They stop sweating. They may die.
6. in 2003
7. 2008
8. 15 days
9. 2023
10. Answers will vary.

Page 60 Grammar & Punctuation

1. Heatwaves usually occur in summer when the air and ground is extremely hot.
2. It can last for days if there is no wind.
3. People may suffer heatstroke when they get too hot.
4. Heatwaves can cause bushfires that destroy large areas of land and property.
5. We can expect more severe heatwaves as temperatures continue to rise across the world.
6. S can have
7. X are, is
8. S are
9. C use, can cause
10. X is, can last

11 – 15 Answers will vary.

16 August, Europe, March, Adelaide

Page 61 Phonic & Word Knowledge

1. firefighter
2. bushfire
3. firecracker
4. campfire
5. firefly
6. SH
7. Z
8. Z
9. S
10. SH
11. S
12. S
13. Z
14. SH
15. bubble
16. people
17. turtle
18. puddle
19. whistle
20. table
21. decoration – an ornament or trimming to beautify
22. potion – a liquid mixture
23. vacation – a holiday
24. education – learning
25. emotion – feelings

Unit 15

Page 63 Reading & Comprehension

1 S	2 P	A	C	E	S	H	3 I	P		4 C		
	O						N		5 G	U	S	6 T
	R						V			R		R
	7 T	R	O	U	8 B	L	E		9 V	I	N	E
10 U					R		S			O		E
N		11 C			O		T			U		S
12 F	O	R	E	S	T		I			S		
A		A			H		G				13 S	
I		T			E		14 A	L	O	N	E	
R		E			R		T				E	
		R				15 R	E	D	D	I	S	H

Page 64 Grammar & Punctuation

1. "You are not coming," says Tor firmly.
2. "It's not fair," Cha grumbles.
3. "I wonder what that is," says Cha to himself.
4. "I know," thinks Cha. "I'll give Cass some flowers."
5. "Now I really am in trouble," Cha mutters.
6. pleaded
7. whispered
8. commanded
9. asked
10. muttered
11. They move carefully among the rocks and craters and (they) soon disappear into the Gravalon Crater.
12. A gust of wind picks him up and (it) carries him into a forest.
13. He grabs a vine and (he) starts to climb.
14. He scurries down and (he) escapes out of the forest.
15. The spaceship has disappeared and (it) is nowhere in sight.

Page 65 Phonic & Word Knowledge

1. steps
2. craters
3. bushes
4. noises
5. rocks
6. grasses
7. forests
8. ferns
9. buzzes
10. gusts
11. reddish
12. bookish
13. dryish
14. boyish
15. biggish
16. strongish
17. bookish
18. reddish
19. strongish
20. biggish
21. u
22. ou
23. u
24. u
25. ou

Unit 16

Pages 66–69 TV show review

Answers will vary.

Term 2 Review

Page 70 Reading & Comprehension

1. First Nations Australians
2. for thousands of years
3. eucalyptus
4. a wing
5. return to the thrower
6. sun protection
7. in the nineteenth century
8. returning home
9. Boomerang
10. a medal

Page 71 Grammar & Punctuation

1. S have made
2. X returns, is thrown
3. C fly, may kill
4. S are used
5. X arrived, saw, described
6. S became
7. S are made
8. X used, would take
9. X was designed, built, was named
10. C were called, received
11. have
12. comes
13. is
14. are
15. make
16. T First Nations Australians have made boomerangs for thousands of years.
17. H Boomerangs are made from the curved root of a tree.
18. H Other types of boomerangs are designed to fly in a straight line.
19. T After their arrival in Australia, British people wanted boomerangs as souvenirs.
20. T They became popular souvenirs in the nineteenth century.
21. They, First Nations Australians
22. They, boomerangs
23. It, boomerang
24. You, everyone
25. who, people
26. can
27. must
28. will
29. might
30. should
31. D
32. T
33. S
34. T
35. S
36. S
37. D
38. T
39. D

ANSWERS

TARGETING ENGLISH HOMEWORK YEAR 4 © PASCAL PRESS ISBN 978 1 925726 61 9

Answers

Page 72 Grammar & Punctuation (cont.)

40 Boomerangs are made from a curved root.
41 A souvenir boomerang can be bought in a shop.
42 Other throwing sticks fly in a straight line.
43 Boomerangs are used as clapping sticks sometimes.
44 The first British people arrived in Australia in 1778.
45 Boomerangs are made by First Nations Australians.
46 Boomerangs have been made by First Nations Australians for thousands of years.
47 The first British people were fascinated by boomerangs.
48 The boomerang was designed and made in Australia in World War I.
49 "I am learning to throw a boomerang so it will come back," said Jai.
50 "Watch out!" called Tan as the boomerang swung round.

Page 72 Phonic & Word Knowledge

1 plane, straight, they
2 people, tree, receive
3 type, flights, design
4 throw, hotels, only
5 use, popular, new
6 boomerang, root, souvenirs
7 saw, fought, for
8 thousands, now, houses

Page 73 Phonic & Word Knowledge (cont.)

9 mul + ga (a)
10 sym + bol (o)
11 hou + ses (e)
12 med + al (a)
13 d
14 id
15 d
16 t
17 id
18 d
19 t
20 id
21 t
22 fought
23 for
24 would
25 their
26 made
27 made, making
28 shaped, shaping
29 threw, throwing
30 returned, returning
31 flew, flying
32 used, using
33 fought, fighting
34 Z
35 S
36 Z
37 SH
38 SH
39 Z
40 S
41 S
42 SH
43 roots
44 trees
45 grasses
46 bushes
47 boomerangs
48 types
49 sticks
50 planes
51 medals
52 thousands

Term 3

Unit 17

Page 75 Reading & Comprehension

1 the Cook Islands
2 Ina
3 She was tired.
4 Her friend lived there.
5 coconuts
6 on the shark's dorsal fin
7 on the shark's head
8 She hadn't asked permission to crack the coconut on his head.
9 leave the sharks alone
10 because Ina cracked a coconut on the shark's head

Page 76 Grammar & Punctuation

1 S A long time ago, there lived a beautiful girl named Ina.
2 C She loved a boy named Tinirau, but he lived on a distant island.
3 S Ina decided to swim to him.
4 C Ina had coconuts with her, but she couldn't open them.
5 X The shark was about to eat Ina when the king of all sharks rose from the sea.
6 C I will take you to Tinirau's island, but you must leave my sharks alone.
7 X Ina got thirsty while she was riding on the shark's back.
8 X It would be a long time before Ina got to Tinirau's island.
9 S To this day, the bump on the top of a shark's head is called Ina's bump.
10 C Ina cracked the coconut and she drank the delicious milk.
11 T A long time ago, there lived a beautiful girl named Ina.
12 P Tinirau lived on a distant island.
13 P She decided to swim to him.
14 T After swimming for a long time, Ina became tired.
15 W Ina took some coconuts for the journey.
16 P Ina cracked a coconut on the shark's dorsal fin.
17 P The shark tossed her off his back.
18 W Tekea the Great saved Ina from the shark.
19 H The shark carried Ina on his back.
20 P The bump on the top of a shark's head is called Ina's bump.
21 W Ina decided to swim to him because he lived on a distant island.
22 T After Ina had been swimming for a long time, she was very tired.
23 T He was about to eat her when Tekea the Great rose out of the sea.
24 W Because she hadn't asked, the shark tossed her off his back.

Page 77 Phonic & Word Knowledge

1 beautiful
2 careful
3 flavourful
4 cheerful
5 skillful
6 peaceful
7 cupful
8 doubtful
9 mindful
10 wonderful
11 flavourful
12 careful
13 doubtful
14 wonderful
15 mindful
16 C couldn't
17 P shark's
18 P Tinirau's
19 C You're
20 C I'll
21 C mustn't
22 P Ina's
23 couldn't = could + not
24 you're = you + are
25 I'll = I + will
26 mustn't = must + not

Unit 18

Page 79 Reading & Comprehension

1 Rock engravings in South Australia are that old.
2 People from Indonesia
3 Willian Jansz
4 No. They resisted the takeover of their land.
5 No. There were wars as some First Nations Australians resisted the takeover of their land.
6 1869
7 1969
8 1976
9 Australia was never an "empty land".
10 "Sorry."

Page 80 Grammar & Punctuation

1 traded, trading
2 claimed, claiming
3 began, beginning
4 said, saying
5 allowed, allowing
6 show; Rock engravings in South Australia showed that the land was inhabited.
7 lands; The First Fleet landed in Port Jackson.
8 becomes; Australia became a Federation.
9 recognises; The Australian Government recognised Aboriginal land ownership.
10 apologises; The Prime Minister apologised to the Stolen Generations.
11 – 15 People: First Nations Australians, William Jansz, James Cook, Tasmanian Aboriginals, Protectors of Aborigines, Governor of Victoria, Jandamarra, Prime Minister, Stolen Generations

ANSWERS

Answers

16 – 20 Places: South Australia, Indonesia, Cape York, Australia, Great Britain, Port Jackson, Tasmania, Flinders Island, NSW, West Kimberley, Western Australia

21 – 25 Objects: First Fleet, British Parliament, Constitution, Australian Government, High Court

26 – 30 Events: First Fleet, Black Wars, Federation, "Mabo" case

Page 81 Phonic & Word Knowledge

1 constitution – j constitute
2 recommendation – f recommend
3 recognition – g recognise
4 decision – h decide
5 reservation – a reserve
6 protection – b protect
7 federations – d federate
8 colonisation – c colonise
9 communication – e communicate
10 education – i educate
11 4 con + sti + tu + tion
12 4 fed + er + a + tion
13 3 pro + tec + tion
14 5 com + mun + i + ca + tion
15 5 col + on + i + sa +tion
16 3 de + cis + ion
17 explorer
18 trader
19 coloniser
20 resister
21 governor
22 protector
23 survivor
24 supervisor

Unit 19

Page 83 Reading & Comprehension

1 The Dragon Slayer
2 in the Dragon's valley
3 Prince Fretalot
4 Prince Fretalot has been sent to slay the dragon because it set fire to the village.
5 Sir Shmelly, Sir Hardbottom, Sir Blunt
6 No. It was the wrong dragon. The dragon only stole pumpkins. It's father set fire to the village.
7 because he's a vegetarian
8 stole pumpkins
9 He offered them some pumpkin soup.
10 Answers will vary e.g. Yes. They will come back for more soup.

Page 84 Grammar & Punctuation

1 – 22 Answers may vary.

1 "Dragon! Prepare to meet your doom," Prince Fretalot cried.
2 "Now hold on a minute," said the dragon. "What appears to be the problem?"
3 "Aren't you the dragon that set fire to the village?" asked Sir Blunt.
4 Sir Shmelly sighed, "It does smell delicious."
5 "Be silent, worm! Your days of mayhem are over," Sir Hardbottom bellowed.
6 Prince Fretalot told Sir Shmelly to be ready to unleash his worst.
7 The dragon said that his father didn't like him much because he'd become a vegetarian.
8 Sir Blunt asked if the dragon had set fire to the village.
9 Sir Shmelly said that it smelled delicious.
10 Sir Hardbottom said that it would be a shame to waste all those pumpkins.
11 kill
12 cooking
13 method
14 release
15 tradition
16 issue
17 protect
18 praise
19 going
20 calm
21 enemies
22 foul

Page 85 Phonic & Word Knowledge

1 b
2 e
3 a
4 f
5 d
6 c
7 princes
8 princesses
9 knights
10 flames
11 grasses
12 valleys
13 pumpkins
14 fish
15 ladies
16 dragons
17 P Dragon's
18 C Let's
19 C Aren't
20 P dragon's; C didn't
21 let + us
22 I + will
23 do + not
24 does + not
25 you + are
26 they + have
27 gnat
28 gnu
29 knee
30 gnome
31 knife
32 knot
33 knitting
34 knight
35 night
36 some
37 not
38 know

Unit 20

Page 87 Reading & Comprehension

1 a student
2 How teachers should treat students.
3 report the teacher
4 Many teachers don't know how to be good teachers.
5 grumpy teachers
6 someone who is patient and kind
7 Yes. The writer gave her an A+ for everything.
8 Answers may vary.
9 They are patient and kind.
10 Answers may vary.

Page 88 Grammar & Punctuation

1 always, have to do, good
2 about time, need to do, good
3 good, kind, always, especially
4 good, never
5 good, patient, every time
6 I think
7 the best
8 I believe
9 I tend to think
10 in my opinion
11 kind
12 patient
13 respectful
14 unkind
15 impatient
16 disrespectful

17 Grumpy teachers who don't like kids never make good teachers.
18 A good teacher never gets cross with a kid who makes a mistake.
19 It's always the teachers who tell kids what to do.
20 I wrote a report that gave my teacher an A+.

Page 89 Phonic & Word Knowledge

1 patient
2 sugar
3 action
4 especially
5 ocean
6 mansion
7 anxious
8 shirt

9 – 13 ghost, ghoul, ghastly, ghetto, Ghana
14 – 18 laugh, enough, cough, tough, rough
19 – 23 high, naughty, eight, sigh, sleigh
24 – 27 being, telling, getting, forgetting, going, everything

Unit 21

Page 91 Reading & Comprehension

1 stories told by First Nations Australians
2 First Nations Australian Elders
3 for thousands of years
4 why Europeans came to Australia
5 stars, mountains, river
6 through stories, dance and art
7 between First Nations Australians and the land
8 It gives them their spirituality as well as food and shelter.
9 No. Many communities have their own language and their own Dreaming stories.
10 Answers will vary.

Page 92 Grammar & Punctuation

1 Dreaming stories explain why birds, animals and people appear and behave the way they do.
2 Dreaming stories explain how natural features such as stars, mountains and other landforms came to exist where they are today.
3 Dreaming stories explain how people should behave towards each other and what happens when people do not follow the rules.
4 Dreaming stories (This is the introductory phrase.)
5 • have been told for tens of thousands of years (first bullet point)

ANSWERS

TARGETING ENGLISH HOMEWORK YEAR 4 © PASCAL PRESS ISBN 978 1 925726 61 9

6 • were never written down (second bullet point)
7 • were told through stories, dance and art (third bullet point)
8 • belong to the entire community of First Nations Australians (fourth bullet point)
9 P Dreaming stories are told through stories, dance and art.
10 P Dreaming stories are told by the Elders to younger members of their communities.
11 C Dreaming stories are diverse because there are many different communities of First Nations Australians.
12 C Dreaming stories tell what happens when people don't follow the rules.

Page 93 Phonic & Word Knowledge

1 Australians
2 persons/people
3 animals
4 stories
5 thousands
6 identities
7 classes
8 stars
9 rules
10 communities
11 S
12 Z
13 S
14 Z
15 Z
16 Z
17 Z
18 S
19 S
20 landforms
21 landfill
22 landfall
23 landmark
24 landowner
25 landslide
26 landscape
27 landmass
28 landward
29 landlord
30 landforms
31 landslide
32 landscape
33 landfall
34 landlord
35 landmark

36 – 39 rapture, culture, nurture, future
40 – 43 cure, secure, sure, insure

Unit 22

Page 95 Reading & Comprehension

1 gravity
2 keeps us on Earth's surface; pulls us towards the centre of the Earth; makes everything fall back to Earth
3 objects with mass
4 objects with more mass
5 the Sun
6 Earth's gravity
7 in its core
8 in a straight line
9 force
10 none of the above

Page 96 Grammar & Punctuation

1 That is a true statement because gravity affects everything on Earth.
2 Gravity makes your feet hit the floor after you jump.
3 Although it may be smaller, an object with more mass has a stronger gravitational force.
4 Because Earth is shaped like a sphere, its centre of mass is located in its core.
5 When you swing on a swing, the seat stops you from falling.

6 – 10 after, and, because, however, in addition

11 c
12 a
13 e
14 b
15 d
16 will be
17 is orbiting
18 have heard; goes; must come
19 is located
20 can change

Page 97 Phonic & Word Knowledge

1 orbit = or + bit (i)
2 statement = state + ment (e)
3 cricket = crick + et (e)
4 surface = sur + face (a/e)
5 even = e + ven (e)
6 reason = rea + son (o)
7 around = a + round (a)
8 gravity = grav + i + ty (i)
9 powerful = pow + er + ful (er)
10 located = lo + ca + ted (e)

11 straight
12 change
13 space
14 shape
15 eight
16 forth
17 ball
18 force
19 more
20 core
21 straight
22 eight
23 main
24 fourth
25 ball
26 weigh

Unit 23

Page 99 Reading & Comprehension

1 V	U	2 L	C	H	A		3 L	E	D	G	4 E	
		A									N	
		I			5 C					6 T	O	R
	7 G	R	A	V	A	L	O	N			R	
					S						M	
	8 M	Y	L	O	S		9 W	E	A	P	O	N
					I						U	
10 D	11 R	A	G	O	N		12 C	L	A	13 W	S	
	E				I		A			A		
	D						V			L		
			14 S	I	L	V	E	R		L		

Page 100 Grammar & Punctuation

1 "One of these must be Vulcha's lair," Tor calls.
2 "Sh-sh!" says Cassini.
3 "The king says it's on a ledge," whispers Tor.
4 "I'll meet you around the other side," suggests Cassini.
5 "Oh, no!" grumbles Tor. "We're trapped."
6 They – Tor and Cassini
7 he – Tor
8 He – the king
9 I'll, she – Cassini
10 it – the dragon
11 the
12 his
13 a, the
14 a, the
15 their
16 her
17 its
18 The
19 – 28 Answers may vary.

Page 101 Phonic & Word Knowledge

1 P Vulcha's
2 C I'll
3 C There's
4 P dragon's
5 C can't
6 P Tor's
7 C Tor's
8 P dragon's
9 P Cassini's
10 C couldn't
11 they are
12 does not
13 could have
14 there is
15 you have
16 you are

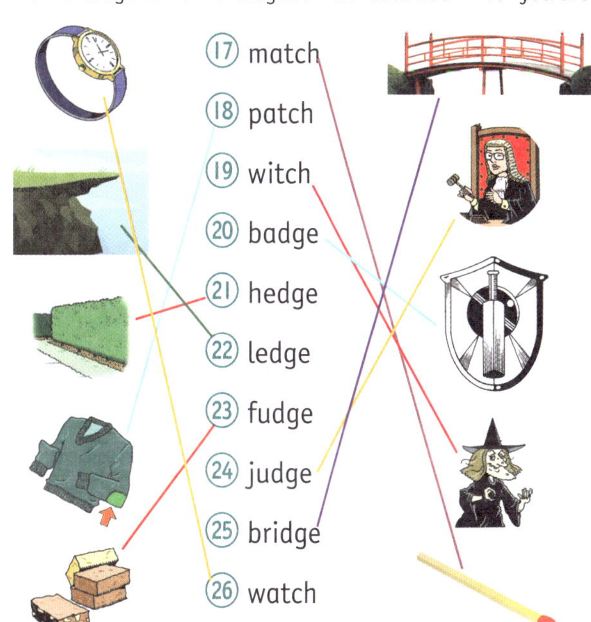

ANSWERS

Answers

27 ledge
28 watch
29 bridge
30 badge
31 match
32 judge
33 brush
34 gush
35 rush
36 push
37 blush
38 crush
39 flush
40 bush
41 mush
42 – 43 push, bush

Unit 24

Pages 102–105 Movie review

Answers will vary.

Term 3 Review

Page 106 Reading & Comprehension

1 rest, relaxation, exercise
2 exercise and rest
3 sleep
4 You rest your brain. You rest your muscles. You replenish your energy sources.
5 10–11 hours
6 You may feel tired. You may be irritable. You may be unable to think clearly. You may get sick.
7 It helps keep you from getting sick.
8 less than hours
9 electronic games, go for a walk, go for a bike ride, go to the park
10 Answers will vary.

Page 107 Grammar & Punctuation

1 S Rest and relaxation are important for growing bodies.
2 C You rest your brain and muscles and replenish your energy sources.
3 X When your body doesn't get enough hours of rest, you may feel tired or irritable.
4 C For relaxation, some electronic games or TV is fine, but limit this to less than hours of 'screen time' per day.
5 S Do some fun activities with your family instead.
6 W For relaxation, some electronic games or TV is fine.
7 T Go for walks with your family after dinner.
8 H Your immune system helps keep you from getting sick.
9 P You could ride your bike to the park.
10 T You should try to put some fun physical activities into your day.
11 T When your body doesn't get enough hours of rest, you may feel tired or irritable.
12 W You may be unable to think clearly if you haven't had enough sleep.
13 W You need 10–11 hours of sleep each night so your body and mind rest.
14 W You shouldn't play electronic games for too long because you need physical activity too.
15 W Although Anna loved playing video games, she knew she should ride her bike more.
16 needed, needing
17 balanced, balancing
18 slept, sleeping
19 rested, resting
20 believed, believing
21 Australia
22 Stayin' Alive Fitness Centre
23 Anzac Day
24 On the Road Bicycles
25 Parkside Road

Page 108 Grammar & Punctuation (cont.)

26 "Turn off the TV now," said Mum.
27 "Can't I watch just more minutes?" begged Anna.
28 "Okay," said Mum. "Just more minutes. Then we'll go to the park."
29 "Can I ride my bike?" asked Anna.
30 "Sure," said Mum. "Let's all ride our bikes."
31 – 35 Answers may vary, e.g.
31 relax, exercise
32 sleepy, alert
33 think, doubt
34 ill, well
35 small, big
36 important
37 needs
38 best, proper
39 clearly
40 some, fine
41 too, little, your, immune
42 tired, irritable
43 electronic, fine
44 some, fun, physical, your

Page 108 Phonic & Word Knowledge

1 doesn't
2 I'd
3 can't
4 you're
5 we'd
6 don't
7 haven't
8 she's
9 could've
10 couldn't
11 c
12 d
13 e
14 a
15 b
16 bal + ance (a)
17 en + er + gy (er)
18 tir + ed (e)
19 pro + per (er)
20 chil + dren (e)
21 lim + it (i)

Page 109 Phonic & Word Knowledge (cont.)

22 bodies
23 researchers
24 games
25 exercises
26 illnesses
27 activities
28 gnome
29 know
30 knead
31 gnat
32 Their, There
33 two, too
34 kneed, need
35 you're, your

36 – 42 should, especially, sugary, special, anxious, ocean, shirt

43 – 50 ghost, laugh, eight ✓, high ✓, rough, ghoul, sleigh ✓, cough

51 S
52 Z
53 S
54 Z
55 S
56 Z

57 – 68 bo**dy**, n**ee**ds, sl**ee**p, r**e**plenish, energ**y**, b**e**, cl**ea**rl**y** (there are 2 here), r**e**searchers, beli**e**ve, sl**ee**p, k**ee**p

69 – 75 weigh, brain, may, able, holiday, relaxation, take

Term 4

Unit 25

Page 111 Reading & Comprehension

1 at the beach
2 Jake
3 sad, angry
4 His dad left. He hates the sea. They had to move house. He doesn't have any friernds.
5 No. Her mouth smiled but she looked sad.
6 He didn't want to talk to anyone.
7 The waves were too big to swim in. He couldn't surf.
8 He wanted the boy to go away.
9 He offered to teach Jake to surf.
10 Answers may vary.

Page 112 Grammar & Punctuation

1 "We'll live by the sea with your grandparents," said Jake's Mum.
2 "What's wrong with you?" said a voice.
3 "I can teach you – if you want to learn," said the boy.
4 "Really? You'll teach me?" asked Jake.
5 "You can have this wetsuit," said Sully, "and I've got an old bodyboard you can have too."
6 He, Jake
7 We'll, Jake and his mum
8 they, Jake and his mum
9 it, the voice
10 you, Jake
11 his, Jake
12 your, Jake
13 Her, mum
14 my, Sully
15 your, Sully
16 – 21 Then, so, And now, Suddenly, Then
22 liked
23 sad
24 frowned
25 enemies
26 younger
27 answer

Page 113 Phonic & Word Knowledge

1 everything = every + thing
2 grandparents = grand + parents
3 nowhere = no + where
4 wetsuit = wet + suit
5 bodyboard = body + board

ANSWERS

TARGETING ENGLISH HOMEWORK YEAR 4 © PASCAL PRESS ISBN 978 1 925726 61 9

Answers

6 B 9 B 12 B 15 T 18 boy
7 B 10 D 13 B 16 know 19 hear
8 B 11 D 14 B 17 where 20 heard

21 – 23 surf, waves, strange
24 – 26 question, nowhere, wetsuit
27 – 29 bodyboard, grandparents, suddenly
30 hat + ed
31 hap + py
32 sud + den
33 pa + rents
34 a + round
35 did + n't

Unit 26

Page 115 Reading & Comprehension

1 an item of food
2 a tool to use
3 a way to do things
4 cut into cubes
5 vegetable stock
6 to blend the mixture
7 fry the onions
8 cook on a low heat
9 30 minutes
10 in an insulated container

Page 116 Grammar & Punctuation

1 oats 3 eggs 5 dates 7 milk
2 bananas 4 seeds 6 baking powder

8 toppings e.g. blueberries, raspberries, date slices, chopped nuts
9 – 15 tablespoon, knife, chopping board, potato peeler, garlic press, teaspoon, cup measure
16 – 27 heat, fry, add, stir, season, Bring, turn, simmer, remove, cool, blend, serve
28 I heated the oil and fried the onions gently.
29 I added 2 cups of stock and 2 cups of water.
30 I turned the heat to low as soon as the soup was boiling.
31 I served it warm with soft bread rolls.

Page 117 Phonic & Word Knowledge

1 mixture
2 picture
3 texture
4 puncture
5 adventure
6 U onions
7 D oil
8 L open
9 S often
10 W one
11 L omit
12 U oven
13 D or
14 W once
15 S of
16 chopped, chopping
17 cooked, cooking
18 heated, heating
19 fried, frying
20 removed, removing

Unit 27

Page 119 Reading & Comprehension

1 The Attraction of Levitation
2 H. G. Paine
3 gravity, riding sleds
4 Johnny Frost
5 Sleds are heavy to drag uphill.
6 Sir Isaac Newton
7 if Sir Isaac Newton reversed his law
8 You can swiftly coast downhill as if the sleds had wings. When you go uphill, the sleds are heavy and feel like they are made of lead.
9 No. It is always easier to go downhill because of gravity. Sir Isaac Newton only named it.
10 I would explain gravity.

Page 120 Grammar & Punctuation

1 – 4 Answers may vary, e.g.
1 When you slowly climb uphill, you have to drag your sled.
2 And all because of an Englishman named Sir Isaac Newton.
3 If he had changed his law, it would be easy for people to go uphill.
4 Then it would be fun to coast.
5 Down the hill you swiftly coast
6 "Oh dear!" little Johnny Frosh sighed sadly.
7 Newton should reverse his law so folks could coast uphill.
8 Little Johnny Frost dragged his sled very slowly up the hill.
9 You can coast like a breeze down the hill.
10 I always think it would be fun to fly with wings.

11 downhill
12 heavy
13 coast
14 swiftly
15 different
16 worse
17 swiftly
18 think
19 drag
20 really
21 named
22 reversed
23 different, light, heavy
24 Englishman, famed
25 pleasure, fun, drag
26 better

27 Answers may vary.

Page 121 Phonic & Word Knowledge

1 should
2 folks
3 would
4 walk
5 half
6 wings e.g. sings, brings, rings
7 lead e.g. bed, red, said
8 famed e.g. blamed, claimed, flamed
9 boast e.g. roast, ghost, toast
10 trick e.g. sick, flick, pick
11 S
12 L
13 S
14 L
15 S
16 read
17 L
18 L
19 lead
20 L
21 S
22 L
23 – 26 dear, seems, made, wood

Unit 28

Page 123 Reading & Comprehension

1 components and instructions for building a pet robot
2 Robobuild
3 children years and older
4 They might choke on small pieces.
5 its price
6 a battery
7 with a remote control
8 No
9 Answers may vary e.g. parents and grandparents as gifts for children.
10 Answers may vary.

Page 124 Grammar & Punctuation

Answers 1 to 4 will be presented as a list without commas.
1 Bowling, Arcade Games, Laser Tag, Dodgems
2 toothbrush, toothpaste, pyjamas, book
3 guitar, music, white shirt, comb
4 Games, T-shirts, Bags, Merchandise
5 When you go to the beach, you need to take your togs, a towel, a hat and sunscreen.
6 At the resort, we could swim in the pool, climb on the fort, watch a movie and play tennis.
7 At school, we do English, maths, science, art and PE.
8 I have dance lessons after school on Monday, Wednesday and Friday.
9 My favourite fruits are strawberries, watermelon, peach, plums and apples.
10 blocks, wheels, caterpillar tracks, nuts and bolts, spanners, battery pack, easy to follow instructions and much more.
11 – 14 Answers may vary e.g.
11 You can build and create using ROBOBUILD.
12 There are over 400 pieces included in the package.
13 The activity is suitable for both beginners and experts.
14 PET ROBOT was voted the best STEM Kit in 2023.

Page 125 Phonic & Word Knowledge

1 magician
2 artist
3 inventor
4 politician
5 electrician
6 follower
7 instructor
8 physicist
9 librarian
10 beginner
11 biologist
12 dragonologist
13 cheesologist
14 ecologist
15 climatologist
16 c
17 d
18 b
19 e
20 a
21 2 sci + ence
22 3 sci + en + tist
23 4 sci + en + tif + ic
24 5 sci + en + tif + ic + ally

ANSWERS

Answers

Unit 29

Page 127 Reading & Comprehension

1 Danyang-Kunshan Grand Bridge
2 the Guiness World Records
3 164.kilometres
4 steel
5 railway bridge
6 earthquakes, floods, typhoons
7 Sydney Harbour Bridge
8 Macleay Valley Bridge
9 just over 1kilometres
10 Answers will vary.

Page 128 Grammar & Punctuation

1 S holds
2 C is, is
3 X took, cost
4 S worked
5 X was, took
6 J The Danyang-Kunshan Grand Bridge, which is in China, is the longest bridge in the world.
7 V It is an elevated railway bridge that runs between Nanjing and Shanghai.
8 V The Sydney Harbour Bridge was built before the Danyang-Kunshan Grand Bridge was built.
9 V While it was being constructed, about 10,000 people worked on the bridge.
10 V The bridge should last for more than 100 years unless something unexpected happens.
11 – 15 in 2010, before, now, during

Page 129 Phonic & Word Knowledge

1 constructed, constructing, construction, constructor
2 elevated, elevating, elevation, elevator
3 built, building, building, builder
4 designed, designing, design, designer
5 expected, expecting, expectation, expecter
6 supported, supporting, support, supporter
7 construction
8 expecting
9 supported
10 built
11 designer
12 build
13 withstand, b
14 without, e
15 withhold, a
16 within, c
17 withdraw, d
18 3 de + sign + ers
19 4 en + gin + eer + ing
20 3 con + di + tions
21 2 a + mount
22 2 rail + way
23 3 con + struc + tion
24 4 kil + o + me + tres
25 2 lon + gest
26 railway
27 lowland
28 withstand
29 earthquakes

Unit 30

Page 131 Reading & Comprehension

1 when you try something new
2 to keep you safe
3 No
4 road, carpark, steep slopes, pools
5 hat, boots, goggles, sunscreen
6 goggles, lifejacket, batteries
7 at the beach
8 jump on a trampoline, swim at the beach
9 school, trampoline, swimming pool, road
10 Answers may vary.

Page 132 Grammar & Punctuation

1 A Where
2 P What
3 V Am wearing
4 V Will need
5 P Who
Answers will vary e.g.
6 Is it safe to ride here?
7 Have I got my helmet?
8 Am I wearing sunscreen?
9 Do I need knee and elbow pads?
10 Should I have a partner?
11 S I will need a water bottle.
12 Q Do the brakes on my bike work?
13 Q Where is the safest place to play cricket?
14 S It is dangerous to play on the road.
15 Q Have I read the map accurately?
16 wear, wore, wearing
17 know, knowing, will know
18 tried, trying, will try
19 check, checked, will check
20 prepared, preparing, will prepare

Page 133 Phonic & Word Knowledge

1 important
2 before
3 sure
4 board
5 thought
6 ball
7 sport
8 taught
9 sauce
10 or
11 unsafe
12 inactive
13 unimportant
14 unprepared
15 unconcerned
16 inaccurate
17 last
18 old
19 nothing
20 worse
21 after
22 finish
23 safety
24 wrong
25 necessary
26 ready
27 understand
28 action
29 items
30 walkers

31 – 38 anything, playground, checklist, everywhere, within, sunscreen, lifejacket, lifeguard

Unit 31

Page 135 Reading & Comprehension

			1 S	2 I	L	V	E	3 R				4 F
5 L		6 C		M				I				L
E		H		P		7 T	I	G	H	T	L	Y
8 D	R	A	G	O	N			H				
G				S		9 P		T			10 W	
E		11 M	I	S	T	E	R		12 T	O	R	
				I		T					O	
	13 K			B				14 H	O	R	N	S
	E			15 L	A	S	S	O			G	
	16 V	I	N	E				P				
	A				17 K	N	E	E	S			

Page 136 Grammar & Punctuation

1 Suddenly a voice cries, "Oh, no you don't, mister!"
2 "There's the silver ball!" he shouts.
3 "We meet in the wrong place again," says Cassini.
4 "Can I keep him for a pet?" asks Cha.
5 "I'll call him Keva," says Cha.
6 shouted
7 asked
8 said
9 whispered
10 commanded
11 "Stop right there!" yelled Cha.
12 "How did you get here?" asked Cassini.
13 "You got here at just the right time," said Tor.
14 "I'm going to keep the dragon for a pet," announced Cha.
15 "I like my new name, Keva," said the dragon.
16 possible
17 under
18 away
19 here
20 roughly
21 release
22 push
23 trap
24 close
25 raises

Page 137 Phonic & Word Knowledge

1 sparkle = spark + le
2 dragon = dra + gon
3 mister = mis + ter
4 over = o + ver
5 lower = low + er
6 silver = sil + ver
7 crater = cra + ter
8 lasso = las + so
9 escape = es + cape
10 Keva = Ke + va
11 a + round
12 gent + ly
13 fly + ing
14 hold + ing
15 a + gain
16 knob + bly
17 – 20 Cassini, Gravalon, impossible, suddenly, releasing
21 – 27 and, the, in, lands, as, on, have
28 – 34 Tor, are, by, seems, no, voice, cries
35 places
36 craters
37 vines
38 bushes
39 sparkles
40 dragons
41 voices
42 grasses
43 walls
44 ledges

ANSWERS

TARGETING ENGLISH HOMEWORK YEAR 4 © PASCAL PRESS ISBN 978 1 925726 61 9

Answers

Unit 32

Pages 138–141 App review

Answers will vary.

Term 4 Review

Page 142 Reading & Comprehension

1 learning to bodyboard
2 Jake
3 at the beach
4 a wetsuit and a bodyboard
5 The wetsuit was tight.
6 to stop the water getting in
7 He hadn't been surfing before.
8 which waves are best
9 excited, proud, eager to go again
10 Answers will vary.

Page 143 Grammar & Punctuation

1 "Those waves look enormous," said Jake under his breath.
2 "We will take it easy today," said Sully.
3 "You have to learn which waves are best," explained Sully.
4 "Jump!" shouted Sully.
5 "I did it!" explained Jake proudly.
6 he, Sully
7 it, wetsuit
8 he, Jake
9 They, Sully and Jake
10 it, surfing
11 Jake met Sully at (the) beach.
12 Sully gave Jake (an) old bodyboard.
13 Sully tied it to (his) wrist with elastic.
14 Jake had to learn (which) waves were best.
15 Sully waved. "You're (a) surfer now!"
16 learn
17 brave
18 worst
19 new
20 hard
21 behind
22 S
23 Q
24 S
25 C
26 – 27 Jake (met) Sully at the beach for a swimming lesson. P, W
28 Sully (zipped) the wetsuit up tight. H
29 – 30 We (will take) it very easy today. H, T
31 enormous, huge
32 afraid, scared
33 cold, freezing
34 beginner, learner
35 tight, firm

Page 144 Grammar & Punctuation (cont.)

36 When Jake went to the beach, he had a wetsuit, a bodyboard, a towel and some sunscreen.
37 Jake thought the waves were enormous, the sea was cold and the skies were grey.
38 Sully was kind, clever, a good friend and an amazing surfer.
39 C got, zipped
40 S was made
41 X was, held
42 learn, learned, learning
43 show, showing, will show
44 held, holding, will hold
45 say, said, will say
46 raced, racing, will race

Page 144 Phonic & Word Knowledge

1 bodyboard
2 snowboard
3 playsuit
4 spacesuit
5 swimsuit
6 blackboard
7 skateboard
8 cardboard
9 tracksuit
10 surfboard
11 D
12 B
13 T
14 B
15 D
16 B
17 B
18 T
19 T
20 B
21 D
22 T
23 wear
24 made
25 sea
26 which

Page 145 Phonic & Word Knowledge (cont.)

27 (e) + las + tic
28 plas + tic
29 bod + y + board
30 e + nor + (mous)
31 wet + suit
32 sur + (fer)
33 L
34 L
35 L
36 S
37 S
38 S
39 L
40 S
41 L
42 L
43 L
44 L
45 L
46 L
47 may be pronounced either way
48 S
49 S
50 may be pronounced either way
51 – 53 Answers may vary e.g.
51 cold, bold, fold, gold, sold, told
52 teach, reach, peach, leech
53 space, mace, race, lace
54 surfer
55 swimmer
56 teacher
57 mathematician
58 biologist
59 inventor
60 old
61 hard
62 lost
63 tight
64 stop
65 enormous
66 unzip
67 unafraid
68 inactive
69 untie
70 unsafe
71 inaccurate
72 hard
73 enormous
74 afraid
75 stop
76 made
77 tied
78 beaches
79 breaths
80 fish
81 wetsuits
82 waves
83 bodyboards

ANSWERS

TARGETING ENGLISH HOMEWORK YEAR 4 © PASCAL PRESS ISBN 978 1 925726 61 9

ANSWERS

ANSWERS

TARGETING ENGLISH HOMEWORK YEAR 4 © PASCAL PRESS ISBN 978 1 925726 61 9